TEACHING GUIDE FOR INDIAN LITERATURE

PUBLICATION OF THIS BOOK

WAS MADE POSSIBLE BY A FEDERAL GRANT

FROM TITLE IV-B OF THE INDIAN EDUCATION ACT

TEACHING GUIDE FOR INDIAN LITERATURE

Volume I — 1st-8th Grade Reading Level

Containing:

Study Questions   Activities

Tests

Teaching Suggestions   Puzzles

Taxonomic Chart

Readability Graph

Checklists   Forms

Written by

Diana Campbell

Cover Illustration and Graphics by

Fred Bia

Edited by T.L. McCarty

Produced by

Title IV-B Materials Development Project
Rough Rock Demonstration School
Rough Rock, Arizona
1983

International Standard Book Number 0-936008-12-1

FIRST EDITION
Printed in the United States of America

by La Plata Color Printing, Inc.

TABLE OF CONTENTS

INTRODUCTION

When I began teaching English as a second language to Navajo students eight years ago, I looked for high-interest, low-level novels about Indians and teenagers. As I found and started using these books in the classroom, I had to devise materials to go along with them. Eventually the materials and methods I had devised and adapted to help the students with their comprehension and appreciation of the novels evolved into a pattern. This system has proved successful and popular with high school students, and involves the following steps.

    a. determine student's reading level
    b. determine level of novels to be read
    c. choose a novel at the student's *instructional* reading level
    d. introduce the novel
    e. introduce vocabulary
    f. student completes the vocabulary checklist
    g. student completes study questions and reads novel
    h. student participates in reading activities
    i. student takes tests (vocabulary and comprehension)

The student's final grade for a novel is an average of his grades on the study questions, the reading activities completed and the test scores.

The materials and suggestions in this guide can be used in a number of ways. The novel may be part of a larger unit, it may be taught to the entire class, or students may read individual novels and do independent projects. It is hoped that the teacher will learn to use materials in this guide where they are appropriate for the teacher's goals, plans and objectives. It is also hoped that the teacher will add to and adapt existing materials to his or her classroom needs, and that the materials and suggestions given here will enable teachers to create their own materials for subsequent novels.

The guide consists of the following materials for each of 11 novels:

    a. study questions
    b. tests
    c. suggested activities
    d. crossword puzzles

Also included is information on Bloom's Taxonomy, Fry's Readability Graph, suggested reading activities, vocabulary checklist and test forms.

Explanation of the 9-Point System

1. **Determine student's reading level.**
    Three types of reading tests can be given:
    a. *Comprehensive diagnostic reading test* such as the Woodcock Reading Test. These tests must be administered individually, which usually takes 45 minutes to an hour. The test is good for the teacher with a small class of remedial students as it gives separate reading levels for word comprehension, passage comprehension, word attack, spelling and analytic skills. Test scores are divided into easy, mastery, instructional and frustrational levels. It is important that the teacher administer these tests correctly. If you are not qualified to do so, perhaps your school's reading or special education teacher can administer the test.

b. *Quick reading test* such as the Wide Range Achievement Test (WRAT). This test consists of spelling, math and reading sections. The spelling section can be given to a group in 30 minutes. The reading section is administered individually and takes only a few minutes. Scoring is simple.

c. *Informal reading inventory.* Several commercial reading inventories are available (see reference section), all of which quickly assess students' performance in a variety of areas such as phonics, word recognition, learning modalities, decoding, spelling, etc. Some can be administered to a group and all determine a student's instructional reading level.

As a last resort, use the school's diagnostic test score if a test such as the CTBS is given school-wide. As these tests are not always consistently monitored or given to late-comers, I find the above-mentioned, classroom-administered tests to be more accurate. Additionally, the teacher can learn much about a student in the one-on-one testing situation.

2. Determine reading level of novel.

An experienced teacher can estimate if a novel is appropriate for the student. However, a quick approximation can be made with Fry's Readability Graph. Briefly, an average number of syllables and an average number of sentences from three randomly chosen 100-word passages should give an average grade level. For a more accurate reading level assessment, the more complex Spache or Dale-Chall systems can be used. (Fry's is included in this guide.)

3. Assign novel at instructional reading level.

Reading levels can be divided into easy, mastery, instructional and frustrational. If a student reads easily at the 4th grade level, he or she should be reading novels on the 5th to 6th grade level. If the student is asked to read at three or more grade levels above his or her present reading level, the student will be "frustrated." Novels at or below grade level are often used in the teaching of literature (Hemingway writes on the 5th-7th grade levels much of the time) since the focus there is on theme, form and ideas.

Administration of the Woodcock Reading test or an informal reading inventory will give the student's instructional reading level. Periodic testing is advised so students can continually move on to more complex books. The best test, however, is the student. If he or she asks no questions, the book is probably too easy. If the student asks questions every step of the way and stumbles over several words per sentence, it is too hard. If a book isn't working, don't use it!

4. Introduce novel.

Many of the books in this guide have historical backgrounds. In such cases, the teacher may include the book in a thematic unit. For example, units could be built around the study of different tribes, the Navajo Long Walk, Spanish explorers, or theme units such as origin legends, relationships, growing up, values, etc.

The teacher should explain as much as possible the historical background of the book. Show the students the area on a map, tell a little about the tribes involved, explain who is fighting against whom and why. This will not detract from the students' enjoyment of the book. In fact, we often assume students can deduce this sort of information as easily as teachers can, but that is not usually the case.

Clue students into the plot. Don't give the story away, but let them know something about the main character and what conflicts he will face in the story. As students progress through the study questions, you may also consider outlining the main events for them, or ask students to do this as a group.

An ambitious teacher may consider tape recording the novels. Most publishers request written permission for doing this, however. You can play key scenes to introduce students to the novel and reluctant readers will eagerly read along. This is a good activity for students for whom this novel is easy reading.

5. Introduce vocabulary.

Vocabulary is not given for the individual novels here. I believe it is better for the teacher to isolate his or her own vocabulary based on his or her purposes and individual students' needs. For example, you may wish to concentrate on unfamiliar words, word endings, place names, etc. You may wish to go over vocabulary with the entire class or let students pick their own words. It is recommended that not more than 10-12 words per chapter be studied at one time.

6. Vocabulary checklist.

I have developed an individualized version of the ECRI (Exemplary Center for Reading Instruction) mastery teaching method. The method involves seeing, saying, writing, and spelling steps. A vocabulary checklist is included here outlining these steps. This is done before the reading of each chapter. You may provide the students with a stack of flashcards with each vocabulary word on the front and definitions and usage on the back, put them on language master cards, or provide the students with a list of words. I find it more efficient to provide my own definitions for students on the cards as they often get bogged down in the language of the dictionary.

7. Study questions and reading of novel.

Students answer the study questions as they read or when they finish each chapter, and may use the book. Study questions are not meant to be used as busy work. The teacher should remember that students are working at their instructional levels and basic learning is taking place. The teacher should be available at all times to help — with clarification of questions, clues to help students locate information and define words. Wander and check constantly.

Many teachers have gone worksheet-crazy in their desperation to find materials, and when given something like these study questions, often misconstrue their purpose. Do not hand the student a pile of study questions and sit back at your desk. Help students utilize a proper, critically thinking approach to the reading. Encourage them to elaborate and synthesize knowledge. The questions are meant to help you with your students, not take your place!

The study questions in this guide are reproducible, but you may have to reword them to your students' levels if you find yourself continually rewording questions. For printing purposes, adequate space may not have been available for all the questions. In those cases where a longer answer or description is required, the teacher can retype the questions or ask the student to respond on separate paper, on the back of the page, in a notebook, or answer orally.

Students should be encouraged to write their answers in complete sentences, in their own words. For many students there is a tendency to look for one or two key words and to copy from there. The result is an unclear answer and an uncertain understanding of the story. It takes longer to respond in complete sentences, but more learning takes place. If a student is having a problem locating an answer, ask him/her to look at the questions before and after for context clues. If the student is having trouble with nearly every question, recheck the reading level. It may be too difficult.

Above all, don't attempt to use these materials without having read the book yourself first! Encourage students to ask questions, ask for definitions, etc. Use each question as a brief teaching opportunity. For example, if the student says, "What does 'taken captive' mean?" you can provide a definition, synonyms and a brief lesson on tense and parts of speech — all in less than one minute.

8. Reading activities.

Reading activities serve many purposes. They enable students to be creative and use their talents in different areas; they lock in learning by focusing attention on material and bringing new awareness to that material; they foster thinking on a variety of levels, and they are fun.

The activities in this guide are of three types: 1) those specific to each novel; 2) general activities that can be used with any novel, and 3) activities geared to each level of Bloom's Taxonomy.

Bloom has divided thinking into six areas — knowledge, comprehension, application, analysis, synthesis and evaluation. A taxonomic chart is included so teachers may devise their own activities according to level.

Students may select their own activities. If you find students tend to stick to a certain type of activity or level of thinking, you can require certain types of activities or focus on different levels. I have found it useful to make a flexible requirement such as "Pick one activity from the analysis or evaluation level and two from the synthesis level" (I recommend requiring more than one activity if time permits. These are excellent substitues for traditional homework and are more likely to be completed because they are more enjoyable.)

Keep supplies on hand for art-related projects. Secure access to a library or keep reference materials in the classroom, and make audio-visual equipment available to students. For research projects and reports or any writing activity it is wise to give specific instructions according to ability and in accordance with available reference materials.

Be sure to give adequate time for all lessons and activities. One week is usually a sufficient length of time to cover most activities.

9. **Tests.**

Various types of tests are included with the novels and the guide. Questions are on the literal, inferential and evaluative levels of comprehension. Keys are provided for the objective questions only and it is suggested that teachers use their own guidelines for essay questions.

I prefer to test after the activities. Students may score higher on the test if it is given immediately after completing the study questions, but I have found they retain material longer if they have a week to "live" with the book.

The test forms included can be used with any novel. Some of these are especially effective for oral questioning. It is recommended that teachers eventually get into the habit of making up their own tests so that they reflect what was emphasized.

A vocabulary test may be given in conjunction with the novel test. A form is included for this purpose. In case the teacher wishes to try using all nine steps and materials provided, a novel-unit checklist is also provided for that purpose. Students seem to enjoy keeping the checklists up-to-date and it helps them keep organized and on-track. It is also helpful for teachers to note student progress. A similar format can be used to reflect the teacher's own requirements and activities. Both the vocabulary checklist and the novel-unit checklist were adapted from a mastery checklist used by ECRI. Adequate space in the squares enables the teacher to write comments or grades.

This guide is one of two teacher's guides on Indian literature and suggested teaching activities. The second guide contains similar material on novels at a higher reading level.

—Diana Campbell
Rough Rock Demonstration School
Rough Rock, Arizona

August, 1982

FRY'S GRAPH FOR ESTIMATING READABILITY

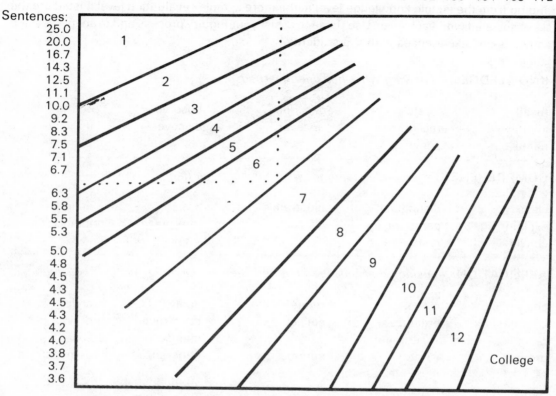

Syllables:

108 112 116 120 124 128 132 136 140 144 148 152 156 164 168 172

Sentences:
25.0
20.0
16.7
14.3
12.5
11.1
10.0
9.2
8.3
7.5
7.1
6.7

6.3
5.8
5.5
5.3

5.0
4.8
4.5
4.3
4.5
4.3
4.2
4.0
3.8
3.7
3.6

Randomly select a 100-word passage. Skip proper nouns, numerals and titles. Count the number of syllables and number of sentences. Do this for three passages in the novel — front, middle and back. Average the figures together and plot on the above chart. If this varies greatly, the text is of uneven readability. If it falls within the shaded areas, grade level is invalid. Readability given is plus or minus one year (i.e., 7th can be 6th-8th grade level).[1]

Sample:

	η of sentences	η of syllables	reading level	true range
passage 1	7.1	134	6	
passage 2	6.3	136	7	
passage 3	6.6	130	6	6-7*
sums	20.0	400	19	
average	(20 ÷ 3 =) 6.7	(400 ÷ 3 =) 134	6.4	5.4-7.4

*= this figure used in guide

[1]From Edward Fry, Rutgers University Reading Center, New Jersey.

BLOOM'S TAXONOMY

Benjamin Bloom, an educator who is now involved with "mastery learning," divides thinking into six areas ranging from the simple knowledge level to the more complex evaluation level. Listed are the types of tasks associated with each level. Use these to assist your inquiry process and to adapt/develop your own activities and experiences with the students.

Simple

KNOWLEDGE — *knowing what has been learned.*

recall	locate	describe	observe	define
identify	recognize	uncover	discover	list
name	show			

COMPREHENSION — *understanding what has been learned.*

classify	distinguish	illustrate	match	estimate
explain	paraphrase	translate	interpret	inquire
convert	restate			

APPLICATION — *using what has been learned.*

chart	model	relate	apply	code
change	organize	collect	construct	draw
report	experiment	use	choose	solve
group	paint	summarize	generalize	demonstrate
sketch	illustrate			

ANALYSIS — *analyzing, figuring out what has been learned.*

categorize	take apart	dissect	parts	analyze
break down	separate	diagram	subdivide	classify
compare	take away	contrast	describe	graph
survey	question	report	hypothesize	generalize
infer	outline			

SYNTHESIS — *creating with what has been learned.*

add to	create	imagine	extend	combine
plan	suppose	modify	predict	devise
hypothesize	design	what if	originate	improve
invent	act	compose	write	

Complex

EVALUATION — *judging what has been learned.*

justify	debate	decide	recommend	solve
appraise	interpret	criticize	consider	judge
conclude	summarize	support	weigh	discriminate
support	critique	evaluate	trial	

General Activities, Tests and Checklists

READING ACTIVITIES

1. Make a list of all the characters in the story and analyze each one. Find a picture that represents or symbolizes that person. Present your work in chart form. o

2. Research a subject, item or idea from the book. o

3. Write several journal entries that three or more of the characters might have written. ★

4. Design a book cover for the book. ★
   - Front cover -- artwork, title, author, etc.
   - Front inside flap -- short summary
   - Back inside flap -- biography of author
   - Back cover -- quotes from "reviews" of the book

5. Write an essay of at least 1000 words discussing the story's themes, plot, major characters, conflicts, setting and author's purpose. Conclude with your opinion of the book. o

6. Conduct a panel discussion with others who have read the same book. Discuss the book's theme or subjects of interest. ∆

7. Make a scrapbook about some subject or the ideas you get from reading the book. ★

8. Make a pamphlet with illustrations or magazine pictures illustrating each chapter. Write a caption or explanation under each one. ★

9. Make a comic book version of the story. ★

10. Make a book of facts you learned while reading the story. ☐

11. Illustrate a scene from the book or draw an item of interest mentioned in the story on a piece of acetate. Project the drawing on a screen and tell the class about it. ☐

12. Make a game to go with the book. Include all parts needed and package in a small box or folder. ★☐

13. Design one or more pages of a newspaper using parts of the story as articles and headlines. ★

14. Write a poem or song about the story, its characters or theme. ★

15. Illustrate six scenes from the story. Use a storyboard format. ★

16. Rewrite the ending of the story. ★

17. Write a play version of the story or part of the story. ★

18. Make up a test for the book and supply an answer key. X

19. Write a short explanation of the conflict of the story and tell what you would have done in the main character's place. X

20. Design a poster advertising the book. ★

21. Design an album cover for the book.
    • Front should include title, performer and artwork.
    • Back should include song titles, liner notes and production info. ★

22. Make a mobile to go with the book. ★□

23. Compare and contrast the book with another book. o

24. Make an illustrated time line for a book with a lot of historical background. X

25. Write a letter to the author. ★ X

26. Make up a new character for the book. Tell what he or she is like. Rewrite one scene in the story, including the new character in it. ★

27. Write or tell what you learned from reading the book. ✓

28. Make a map showing where events in the book took place. X□

29. Make a crossword puzzle for the book. □

30. Write a biography of the author. □

31. Make a collage of the book's theme, or of the main character's interests and personality. ★

32. Write a commercial advertising the book for radio or TV. Record it. ★

33. Do an experiment from the book or do something that was done in the book. □

34. Collect magazine pictures pertaining to the book. Tell about each one as you show them on the opaque projector. X□

35. Fill out a plot chart (form included). o

36. Fill out a character sketch chart (form included). o

37. Write a letter to a friend recommending the book. ★ X

38. Present a vivid oral or written description of an interesting character. X □

39. Prepare a skit and select people to dramatize part of the book. ★

40. Role play a situation with you and your classmates representing characters in the story. ★ Δ

41. "Try" the book by a jury of students. Δ

42. Draw some of the characters on the board and describe each one. □

43. Paint a cigar box to look like a book, with scenes of the story or other pertinent objects inside. □

44. Make a diorama. ★ □

45. Make silhouette stick figures and "act out" the story using the overhead projector or opaque projector. □

46. Play password with four people who have read the same book. Moderator should pass flashcards with words that have to do with the story. X □

47. Record the book or parts of it. □

48. Write your own story based on part of the book. ★

49. Write or tell five things that would make the book better. Δ o

50. Make puppets representing the major characters and act out a scene. □

51. Write a book review of the novel and submit it to the school or city newspaper. o Δ

52. Make models of the book's characters, animals, objects or buildings. Use clay, soap, wood or plaster. ★

53. Make dolls to represent the main characters. Use paper, wire, rags, corn husks, apple cores, etc. ★

54. On large pieces of "butcher" paper hung across one wall, paint a mural depicting important scenes from the book. *

55. Use a map to trace the routes of the characters in the book. Figure out the number of miles you

covered between towns, etc. What is the terrain like? Present your findings in a drawing or tell the information to the teacher or class. X □

56. Build a 3-dimensional scene from the story. □

57. Outline or "diagram" the story on a chart. □o

58. Write a letter from one character to another. Have the other character write back. X ✸

59. Point out parts in the story that show the character has changed. o

60. Give an account of what should have been done had you been one of the characters in a similar situation. o

61. Read from the story orally while others are pantomiming the action. □✸

CHARACTER SKETCH CHART

Name _____

Title _____   Date _____

Name of character	Relationship to main character	Description (physical and personality, emotions)	Age	Importance in plot (What happens to him in story?)
	Main Character			

PLOT CHART

Name_____

Title_____

Date_____

10. Climax:

(Major events leading to climax)

9. _____

8. _____

7. _____

6. _____

5. _____

4. _____

3. _____

2. _____

1. _____

Setting:

Rising action

Falling action

Conclusion

11. _____

12. _____

13. _____

Theme: _____

Conflict: _____

Point of view: _____

TEST 1

Title of Novel _____   Student's Name _____

_____   Date _____

    I. **Spelling**

1.	7.
2.	8.
3.	9.
4.	10.
5.	11.
6.	12.

   II. **Usage**

1.
2.
3.
4.
5.
6.
7.
8.
9.
10.
11.
12.

  III. **Comprehension**

1. Summarize the story.

2. List the characters and briefly tell about each one.

3. What was the main character's conflict? How was it resolved?

4. What was the most interesting part of the story? Why?

TEST 2

Name _____

Title of Novel _____   Date _____

1. List the main events of the story in order.

2. What is the main character's name?

3. Describe him.

4. What is his problem in the story?

5. How is his problem solved?

6. Who are the other characters in the story?

7. Describe two of the other characters.

8. How does the story end?

TEST 3

Title _____   Date _____

1. **SETTING** — Where and when does the story take place? What time period does the story cover?

2. **PLOT** — Give a brief summary of the major events of the story.

3. **CLIMAX** — What is the climax or "big scene" in this novel?

4. **CHARACTERS** — Name the major characters in the story and briefly tell what they did in the story and how they related to or affected the actions of the main character.

5. **CONFLICT** — What problem is the novel or main character concerned with? How is the conflict resolved?

6. **POINT OF VIEW** — Who is telling the story?

7. **THEME** — What is the message of the story? What was the story basically about? What lesson in life does the author want you to experience with the main character?

VOCABULARY TEST

Title _____   Name _____

Author _____   Name _____

I. **Spelling**

1.   6.
2.   7.
3.   8.
4.   9.
5.   10.

II. **Definitions** (Give the meanings for any five of the vocabulary words.)

1.

2.

3.

4.

5.

III. **Usage** (Use the other five vocabulary words in sentences that show you know the meaning of the word.)

1.

2.

3.

4.

5.

IV. **Write 8 sentences about the story using the vocabulary words.**

1.

2.

3.

4.

5.

6.

7.

8.

VOCABULARY CHECKLIST

Name _____

Title _____

Chapter _____

Pre-Steps: Find the flashcards or language master cards that go with the chapter you are now reading in your novel.

Go over the pronunciation of the words on the flashcards with the teacher or listen to the language master cards.

Refer to these cards for definitions and example sentences.

Practice Steps: Vocabulary words

1. Hear the word.

2. Read the word.

3. Spell and read.

4. Read each word part (or syllable) while running your finger under the syllables.

5. Spell each word part and read the word.

6. Look up. Spell and say the word.

7. Spell and read.

8. Write, spell and read 3 times.
   (Say each letter as you write it.)

9. Proof and correct. (Is spelling correct?)

10. Look up. Spell and say.

11. Read or listen to the definition of the word.

12. Look up. Say the definition.

13. Write and say the definition.
    (Say each word as you write it.)

14. Proof and correct.

15. Look up. Say the definition.

16. Read or listen to the word in a sentence.

17. Think of a sentence using the word.

18. Write and say your sentence.

19. Look up. Use the word in a sentence.

20. Lock step:
    Read the word 3 times.
    Spell and say 3 times.
    Say the definition 3 times.
    Say the word in a sentence 3 times.

The teacher has checked & OK'd my notebook for written steps.

NOVEL UNIT CHECKLIST   Name _____

Title						
1. I was present when the teacher introduced the novel and I understand what was said.						
2. I was present when the teacher introduced the vocabulary for each chapter.						
3. I have completed the vocabulary checklist for each chapter and the teacher OK'd my work.						
4. I have read the novel.						
5. I have completed study questions for each chapter of the novel.						
6. I have completed the assigned reading activities.						
7. I have completed extra reading activities.						
8. I have taken the vocabulary test and passed with a score of 80%-100%.						
9. I have taken the comprehension test and passed with a score of 80%-100%.						
Date completed						
10. The teacher agrees that I have completed all projects on this novel and my average grade is:						

Novel Units

ARROW TO THE SUN

Reading Level 1-2

(A Pueblo Indian tale adapted and illustrated by Gerald McDermott. A Puffin Book, by Penquin Books, 625 Madison Ave., New York, NY 10022, 1977. $2.50. ISBN no. 104050.2114.)

This Caldecott Award-winning book is an adaptation of the Pueblo Indian myth which explains how the spirit of the Lord of the Sun was brought to the world of men. A young Peublo maiden gives birth to the Boy who goes in search of his father. A wise man, Arrow Maker, turns him into an arrow and shoots him to the sun, where he undergoes four trials to prove that he is indeed the Child of the Lord of the Sun.

This story is like the origin myths of many cultures in that it features the god-spirit coming before the birth of man, the virgin mother and the trials the child of God must endure. If the class is studying similar tales, the students could compare and contrast the various myths of origin.

The book is beautifully illustrated in an abstract graphics style that lends itself well to students' individual interpretation of the story and illustrations. I have found this an excellent book to use as a model with students who then go on to read and illustrate other myths and legends.

Because of the reading level of this story it is recommended that the questions be used for **oral** class activities and discussion. For instance, one activity is "Read about pueblos." The teacher may read to the students and they will instead, "Listen to some stories about pueblos." The activities can and should be adapted to your class and individual abilities, especially since a wide range of ages will be reading the books.

Additional activities and suggestions can be found in the back of this guide. Use and adapt those that are appropriate for your students.

Questions

1. What did the Lord of the Sun do?
2. Where did the "spark of life" go?
3. What did it become?
4. How was the Boy treated?
5. Why did the Boy leave home?
6. Who are the three people he went to?
7. What did the Arrow Maker tell the Boy?
8. What did he do to the Boy?
9. How did he get to the Sun?
10. What did the Boy say to the Lord of the Sun?
11. What will the Boy have to do to prove he is the Child of the Sun?
12. Does he agree to do this?
13. What is happening in the pictures on the next seven pages?
14. What happened when the Boy came from Kiva of Lightning?
15. What did the father tell his son?
16. How did the Boy get back to earth?
17. Where did he go?
18. What happened when he returned?

Activities

1. Illustrate a scene from the book (e.g. the celebration, being shot to the sun as an arrow or the Boy meeting his father for the first time). Use your own artistic style or try an abstract style such as that used in the book. ☐

2. Study the artist's style of geometric design by looking in some art books. Draw some pictures in this style. **X**☐

3. Read about pueblos. ✓

4. Read some other pueblo tales. ✓

5. Read about some origin legends from different tribes. ✓

6. Tell (the teacher or the class) about an origin legend you are familiar with. **X**☐

7. Make a book (for yourself or for elementary students) in which you retell a myth or legend in your own words and illustrate it. ★ ☐

Crossword Puzzle — *Arrow To the Sun*

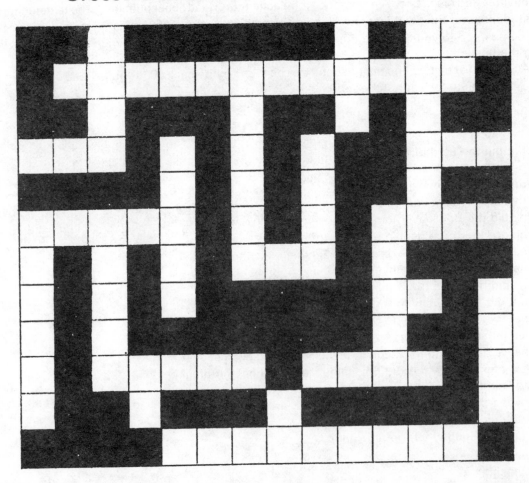

ACROSS

1. The boy asked _____ Maker for help.

4. He sent a spark of life to the earth.

6. The Boy was the Child of the _____ .

9. The Spark of Life became the _____ .

10. Arrow _____ was a very big help.

12. The first person the Boy asked for help.

13. The Spark of Life traveled down a _____ of the sun.

14. The people celebrated the Dance _____ Life.

16. Another name for Serpent.

18. Arrow Maker was a _____ man.

20. When he came from the Kiva of _____ , he was transformed.

DOWN

1. The other children would not let the Boy _____ in their games.

2. He had to pass through this kiva.

3. The spark of life went to a _____ .

5. The Boy wanted to find his _____ .

7. He was turned into an _____ and shot to the sun.

8. Pot Maker was working with _____ .

10. A Pueblo _____ was his mother.

11. He had to pass through four _____ to prove he was the Lord's son.

12. Corn Planter was tending his _____ .

15. There were some of these in the first kiva.

17. If Pot Maker spoke, she might have said _____ .

19. What the Boy might have said to show surprise.

25

NIGHT AT RED MESA

Reading Level 2-3

(An Educational Challenges Production by Harvey W. Paige. McCormick-Mathers Publishing Company, Cincinnati, Ohio 45202, 1975. ISBN no. 0800918886.)

This mystery story takes place on the Navajo reservation at a place called Red Mesa. A teenage boy, Johnny Yazzie, is called home from boarding school by his grandfather. Some strange things have been going on and Peter Yazzie wants his grandson to help solve the mystery. Johnny gives up a summer job on the rodeo circuit to go home where he soon becomes involved in the mysterious Legend of Red Mesa.

This book is excellent for all ages. For the beginning reader, this may be one of his/her first full-length novels with chapters. It is similar in size and type to the Scholastic Double Action high-interest low-level novels. The teenage main character and the mining company villains make this an excellent choice for extremely remedial high school students. They will identify with the contemporary setting, Johnny's love of family and rodeo and the timely issue of the controversial mining companies.

At this level, the teacher may read to the students, students may participate in round-robin style oral reading, or the story can be taped. If this is one of the student's first full-length novel reading experiences, I suggest stopping after every page or so and quizzing students orally for comphension. This also helps get them used to class discussion methods and involves them in solving the mystery.

Since this is a mystery, that makes it a good vehicle for charting plot. Students can collect as they read or outline the plot later.

Another strong point of this book is the dream/legend. Students usually respond readily to discussion of legends and reality vs. unreality. They can look for clues in the story that support their opinions. Some lively responses can be expected from questions about the danger Johnny might be in. Will he kill himself like those in the legend? This is a good point in the book for creative writing suggestions. What legends do the students know about their area? What mysterious happenings do they know about?

Questions

Chapter One

1. What is the main character's name?
2. Where is his home?
3. How many hours has he been on the bus?
4. How much money does he have in his pockets?
5. Where does he go to spend his money?
6. Why is Sam surprised to see Johnny?
7. Who else is in the diner with them?
8. Why does Johnny say that he came home?
9. Where is Johnny's father?
10. What does Johnny hear the two men talking about?
11. What does Frank Benally say when he hears the two men talking?

12. Johnny says his grandfather has been noticing some strange happenings on Red Mesa. What kinds of things have been going on?
13. What did Johnny give up to go home? What summer job had he been offered?
14. Who else has been having trouble with strange happenings?
15. What happens to Johnny's 60¢?
16. How does Johnny feel about having to come home?
17. What does Sam Fife say to cheer him up?
18. How does Frank Benally's warning make you feel?

Chapter Two

1. What is Johnny's grandfather's name?
2. What does he tell Johnny?
3. Who was Noah Lujan?
4. What does grandfather say about coyote?
5. What does Johnny think they should do?
6. What do Johnny and his grandfather argue about?
7. What does grandfather think about the new world?
8. What does Johnny decide to do in the end? Why?

Chapter Three

1. Where did Johnny and his grandfather go? Why?
2. What is the story Peter Yazzie told his grandson about?
3. What effect did the drums have on the young Navajo?
4. What did he see on the top of Red Mesa?
5. What did he do with the body?
6. What happened after that?
7. How does the "story" end?
8. What happens to Johnny Yazzie the next morning?
9. What does Johnny want to do about the drums?
10. What does grandfather say about the idea?
11. How does Johnny feel about what his grandfather says?
12. What does Johnny think about at the end of the chapter?

Chapter Four

1. What led Johnny Yazzie on?
2. Describe Johnny when he reached the top of Red Mesa.
3. Describe what he found.
4. Why did Johnny decide to act out the legend of Red Mesa?
5. What would you do if you were Johnny?
6. What did Johnny discover when he got back to Red Mesa?
7. Do you think Johnny will kill himself? Why or why not?

Chapter Five

1. What did Nancy Yazzie and her younger brother find?
2. What did old Peter Yazzie find out on his own?
3. Why did Peter Yazzie tell his grandchildren to call the police?
4. Why were the two Plains Indians hired by the mining company?
5. Why did the mining company want the Indian land?
6. If it wasn't tricks of Old Man Coyote, then who was causing strange things to happen on the mesa?
7. What was the reason for the Northern Indian killing his companion?
8. How does the story end?

Test

1. Johnny Yazzie has been away at
   a) boarding school
   b) a rodeo
   c) a mining company

2. The diner is owned by
   a) Noah Lujan
   b) Frank Benally
   c) Sam Fife

3. Frank Benally says that the strange happenings on Red Mesa are because of
   a) Coyote
   b) the mining company
   c) Plains Indians

4. Peter Yazzie thinks his grandson should
   a) go back to school
   b) find out what is happening on Red Mesa
   c) stay home and take care of Nancy and her little brother

5. According to the story of Red Mesa, the drums want the hearer to
   a) sacrifice himself
   b) sacrifice someone else
   c) sacrifice a buffalo

6. When Johnny decides to act the legend on Red Mesa, he follows the drums to the top of the mesa and finds
   a) the body of a young Indian
   b) Noah Lujan
   c) a coyote

7. Nancy and her little brother find

    a) the buffalo robe

    b) the lease to the mining company

    c) a box of things used to make the lights and sounds from the mesa

8. The men had played the trick on the Navajos of the area

    a) because they were making a movie

    b) because the mining company wanted the mineral rights to their land

    c) so everyone would think Peter Yazzie had killed Noah Lujan

9. At the end of the story

    a) Johnny goes back to school

    b) Johnny decides to stay home and take care of his little brother and sister until his father comes back

    c) Grandfather tells Johnny to call the rodeo and see if he can still work for the summer

Activities

1. Draw a picture of the diner, Red Mesa or Johnny Yazzie's home (or of some other setting in the story). □

2. Draw pictures of each of the main characters doing something they did or would like to do. (For example, Johnny at a rodeo, Nancy discovering the box or grandfather telling the story of Red Mesa.) □✶

3. Write a letter Johnny might have written to a friend back at school about his summer. ★

4. Do you know a legend concerning your area? Tell or write about it. X □

5. Write a mystery story about the above legend. ★

6. Write a dialogue between the two men from the mining company. ✶

7. Write a letter to the editor of your school or local newspaper about mining rights on the reservation. Should big corporations be getting the profit? Should we be more concerned about our natural resources? △o

8. Research mining. Write a report about mining or mining as a career. X □

9. Compare Red Mesa, Arizona to the Red Mesa in the novel. How are they alike? How are they different? o △

10. Write a report on some aspect of rodeo. X

11. Write a story describing Johnny Yazzie's summer on the rodeo circuit if he hadn't gone home. ★

12. The book contains some beautiful illustrations. Draw your own illustration for one of the scenes. Use your own style. Your drawings don't have to look like those in the book. What do you think the characters look like? ★

13. Write a letter to a mining company. □

14. Pretend you are on the side of the mining company. Justify your actions and position on this issue. o △

15. Role play with your classmates a confrontation between two or more of the characters in the story. o ★

16. Change the story and have something different happen on Red Mesa. ✶

Crossword Puzzle — *Night At Red Mesa*

ACROSS

4. Johnny thought he heard _____ .

6. Peter Yazzie thought there were _____ many strange happenings.

7. "_____ at Red Mesa."

9. The person in the Red Mesa legend is supposed to _____ himself.

11. The color of Johnny's eyes.

12. Johnny's last name.

15. Grandfather thinks all of this is the doing of Trickster _____ .

17. Johnny finds a _____ body on top of the mesa.

18. Sam Fife does not _____ the Red Mesa Mining Company.

21. Near Red Mesa is Pointed _____ .

DOWN

1. Johnny has 60¢ to spend at Fife's _____ .

2. Main character's first name.

3. Johnny is _____ boarding school when his grandfather sent for him.

4. Grandfather does not know what to _____ about the strange happenings.

5. The _____ company hired two Indians to scare people off their land.

8. Frank Benally said something _____ was going on.

10. Noah _____ really died of natural causes.

11. "They won't sell!" cried _____ .

13. The answer to the mystery was found in _____ _____ .

14. What Johnny could be doing.

16. "The Legend of Red _____ ."

18. When Johnny's work was _____, Peter sent him back to rodeoing.

20. At the _____ of the mesa, a buffalo hide was neatly laid out.

22. Peter told his grandchildren to run _____ the trading post to send for the police.

31

KILLER OF DEATH

Reading Level 3-4

(A Dell Yearling Book for young people by Betty Baker. Dell Publishing Co., Inc. 1 Dag Hammarskjold Plaza, New York, NY 10017, 1963. $1.25. ISBN no. 440-044.)

In the mid-1800's there was much activity in the Southwest as the United States and Mexico tried to settle their border dispute. Not the least of these activities were the Apache uprisings. Before the Apaches were moved to reservations in Arizona and New Mexico, they had the run of the Southwest. Mexico agreed to the United State's propositions, but only if the Apaches were removed to north of the new border.

Killer-of-Death takes place during this time of upheaval. Killer-of-death is a young Apache boy coming into manhood. A shaman's son, Gian-nah-tah, becomes his enemy. The two were once friends but are not united again until both have lost nearly everything during the Mexican-American dealings.

Killer-of-Death is a sensitive young man who feels there must be something wrong with him because he has so much compassion for those he is supposed to hate.

There are many interesting aspects to this novel, one being the first person point-of-view of a boy in these times, a boy who is an eager participant in Apache raiding parties.

Teaching emphasis should be on historical background and the values held by a young boy growing up in a time of upheaval. Much discussion can be centered around the raiding parties, his antagonism toward Gian-nah-tah, and his compassion.

This and the following two novels are what might be called "intermediate" readers. These are full-length novels with easy to follow adventure plots, good character development and abundant themes. If the students are inexperienced with essay tests, these are excellent books to use for that purpose.

Questions

Foreword

1. Where did the Mimbreño Apache live?
2. How was the border dispute between Mexico and the United States settled?
3. Why did Mexico enforce the Project of War?
4. How was peace finally achieved?
5. Where do the Mimbreños live today?

Chapter One — The Scent of Big Game

1. What was the narrator's grandfather's life like?
2. What was his father's life like?
3. What was happening when the narrator was a baby?
4. How did his brother die?
5. What did his father do to help the mother get over her grief?
6. What did the narrator call his adopted brother? Why?

7. What happened when the narrator was 12?
8. Why do the narrator and Gian-nah-tah want to kill a deer?
9. How did the narrator trick Lazy Legs?
10. What important news does Lazy Legs have?
11. What happened to Gian-nah-tah?
12. Who is Juan José?
13. Where is the narrator's father going?
14. Why won't he take his son?
15. What does Lazy Legs tease his brother about?
16. Why is Gian-nah-tah angry?
17. How does he show his anger?

Chapter Two — Dance of the Rabbits

1. What is the narrator preparing to do?
2. Who is Shy Maiden?
3. Why did Gian-nah-tah rub his body with mint?
4. Why did the mockingbird stop singing?
5. How does the narrator find game?
6. What did his "four-legged scout" lead him to?
7. What were the rabbits doing?
8. Why did Lazy Legs say they should not kill them?
9. What were the narrator's reasons for thinking it would be all right?
10. Who did they thank? How?
11. What did the Coyote do?

Chapter Three — Victory for the Enemy

1. What did the boys do with the rabbits?
2. What does the little sister like to do?
3. How do people spoil her?
4. What did the boys do?
5. What did Gian-nah-tah do to Lazy Legs?
6. Why do the brothers say he did this?
7. What do people call Gian-nah-tah? Why?
8. What does Gian-nah-tah want to do with his deer?
9. Now that he has a deer, what can he do?
10. What news do the narrator's father and the other men have?
11. What does the narrator do to get strong for the hunt?
12. What does his father give him?

Chapter Four — A Black Thread on the Blanket

1. What did the narrator's father say about the old days?
2. What changes have the "white-eyes" brought according to him?
3. What is the deer-head mask used for?
4. How did the narrator catch his deer?

5. How did he exaggerate his success to the village?
6. Who will get the deerskin?
7. How did the narrator get his name?
8. What is his name?
9. What does he see in the village of Juan José?
10. Who is Red Sleeves?
11. What is his other name?
12. What is the ''blanket''?
13. What will it mean when the blanket is burned?
14. What do father and son see on the way home?
15. What did the whiteman Johnson do?
16. What does this mean to Killer-of-Death?

Chapter Five — In the Deserted Village

1. What did Little One want?
2. How did Lazy Legs hurt his brother's feelings?
3. What did Killer-of-Death do with the gourds?
4. How did he catch the ducks?
5. Who did the footprints belong to?
6. How is Gian-nah-tah cheating?
7. Why did Killer-of-Death take Gian-nah-tah's hidden food supply?
8. How does he know that Lazy Legs knew about Gian-nah-tah's hidden food?

9. What is he afraid Gian-nah-tah will do to get even?

Chapter Six — My Time Comes

1. What did Killer-of-Death take with him for his apprenticeship testing?
2. What happened the first four days?
3. What were some of the hardships he endured?
4. Who was following him?
5. How did he get vengeance for his brother who died long ago?
6. What did he do with the dead rattlesnake?
7. How long was Killer-of-Death gone?
8. What happened when he returned home?
9. Has Gian-nah-tah changed? Did the curse work?
10. What does Killer-of-Death think about this?
11. How did the g'an dance lose its mystery for Killer-of-Death?
12. What else does Killer-of-Death have to do for his apprenticeship?
13. What did Chato do?
14. Did Shy Maiden accept the horses?
15. What raid is Killer-of-Death going on?

Chapter Seven — The First Raid

1. What did the shaman predict?
2. How did the villagers react?
3. Why does Killer-of-Death have ''a crawling feeling'' in his stomach?

4. Who is Child-of-Water?
5. Why did Killer-of-Death ask the turquoise for protection?
6. Describe the raid.
7. What did Killer-of-Death do during the raid?
8. What are his feelings about Red Sash?
9. Why were his people disappointed with the raid?
10. What did Killer-of-Death get out of the raid?
11. What did he give Little One?
12. What do Killer-of-Death and Lazy Legs do?
13. Why does Killer-of-Death want to see the shaman?
14. What "sickness" does he think he has?

Chapter Eight — A Share of the Spoils

1. Who has come to visit?
2. What news does he bring?
3. What does Mangas fear?
4. What plan has he thought of to get rid of the white settlers?
5. What is Broken Nose doing?
6. What honor did Broken Nose give Killer-of-Death?
7. Why did Gian-nah-tah spit on Killer-of-Death?
8. What has Mangas asked of Killer-of-Death?
9. What does Killer-of-Death's father tell him to do while he is gone?
10. What happened to his father the night before?

Chapter Nine — The Enemy Strikes

1. What was going on in the Mexicano town?
2. Why does Killer-of-Death say he will have to be careful?
3. How did Mangas plan to trick the soldiers?
4. What did Gian-nah-tah do?

Chapter Ten — Apache

1. What happened? What condition is Killer-of-Death in?
2. What did he see in the soldier's camp?
3. What happened because of the rain?
4. Describe his journey towards home.
5. Who was there when he woke up?
6. How did he escape the two warriors?

Chapter Eleven — Vengeance

1. Why does Killer-of-Death think he will be a poor warrior?
2. What does Apache mean in Papago?
3. How does Killer-of-Death's family react to seeing him?
4. How does he know Gian-nah-tah had not told his family he had died?

5. Where are Gian-nah-tah and some others from the village?
6. Why does Killer-of-Death want vengeance on Gian-nah-tah?
7. Why are they going to see Juan José?
8. What does Lazy Legs say the white-eyes have been doing?
9. What does Killer-of-Death think of the magic line?
10. Why does he go to the campfire to talk to his father?
11. What does his father tell him about Shy Maiden's father?

Chapter Twelve — We Burn the Blanket

1. Why did Killer-of-Death stay behind while the others went to the village?
2. Who came?
3. What does Gian-nah-tah say about Lazy Legs?
4. Why do they fight?
5. What did Little One have?
6. Where are there other guns?
7. How did the chief die?
8. Describe the attack. What happened to the Apaches? Why?
9. How many survived?
10. Who is left in Killer-of-Death's family?
11. Who is left in Gian-nah-tah's family?
12. What were Killer-of-Death's father's last words?
13. Why were Gian-nah-tah and Killer-of-Death no longer enemies?
14. What did it say in the newspaper that Broken Nose brought back from Tucson?
15. What was Mangas' plan?
16. What happened to Killer-of-Death when peaceful times came again?
17. Why did the white-eyes come to the Mexicano town?
18. What did they do to Mangas? Why?
19. What happened in the Chiricahua Mountains?
20. How did Killer-of-Death's earlier dream come true?
21. How did his father's words come true?

Chapter Thirteen — Among the Ashes

1. What is Killer-of-Death's life like now?
2. What is Gian-nah-tah going to do?
3. How did Gian-nah-tah and Geronimo end up?
4. What does the missionary have to say to Killer-of-Death?
5. What does Killer-of-Death decide? Why?
6. What does the last sentence mean to you?

Test

1. Who is the narrator?

   a) a half-breed adopted by a shaman
   b) a young warrior from a Mexican tribe
   c) a 14-year-old Apache boy

2. Who is Gian-nah-tah?

   a) the shaman's son
   b) the narrator's father
   c) the narrator's brother

3. What did the narrator do that was bad luck?

   a) courted Shy Maiden
   b) shot a deer
   c) trapped and killed some rabbits

4. Who gets to begin his appreticeship testing first?

   a) Killer-of-Death
   b) Gian-nah-tah
   c) Lazy Legs

5. Who gave the narrator his name?

   a) Red Sleeves
   b) his father
   c) Juan José

6. Killer-of-Death has some problems during his testing because

   a) he is afraid
   b) he kept a secret from the shaman
   c) Gian-nah-tah is following him

7. What is Red Sleeves' other name?

   a) Mangas Colorado
   b) Broken Nose
   c) Juan José

8. What did Gian-nah-tah tell the Apaches about Killer-of-Death's behavior during the raid?

   a) that he ran off
   b) that he was brave
   c) that he was killed

9. What is the magic line?

   a) a wall
   b) a road
   c) the Mexican-American border

10. In the end

    a) Apaches successfully killed all attackers

    b) Apaches were moved to a reservation

    c) Geronimo surrendered to the United States soldiers

11. How does Gian-nah-tah make life difficult for Killer-of-Death?

12. List the members of Killer-of-Death's family and tell a little about each one.

13. Why does Killer-of-Death think he is a coward?

14. What did Killer-of-Death have to do to become a warrior?

15. What changes did the white-eyes bring to the Apache way of life?

Activities

1. At the end of Chapter Two, the coyote is laughing. What is the meaning of this, in your opinion? Tell what you know about the trickster coyote in your answer. o

2. Read some coyote stories and report on one. ✓ X

3. Interpret the chapter titles. Some of them are very poetic. Tell how they relate to the story. o

4. Research topics: X ☐
   - Mangas Colorado
   - Geronimo
   - Apaches
   - Mexican-American Border Settlement

5. Compare and contrast manhood ceremonies of different tribes. o

6. Draw character sketches of each character in the story based on descriptions given in the book. ☐

7. Tell how Killer-of-Death lived up to his name. Give yourself a name and tell how you have lived up to your name. ☐ o ✶

8. Make a map showing where events in the book take place. ☐

9. Role play a scene between Gian-nah-tah and Killer-of-Death. ★

10. Write journal entries that three of the following might have written. Show how the three characters might see a situation differently. ★
    - Killer-of-Death, his father, Lazy Legs, Gian-nah-tah, his father, Mangas, Geronimo, Johnson

11. Make a list of reasons that prove the U.S. didn't make a wise settlement with Mexico. o △

12. Compare Gian-nah-tah's trials during his manhood testing with those of the narrator. o

13. Paint a cigar box to look like a cover for the book. Put some important scenes inside and some objects that represent things from the book. ☐

14. Make an illustrated time line of the historical facts presented in the story. X

15. Write letters of apology from Gian-nah-tah to Killer-of-Death. □ ★

16. Write a journal letter the narrator may have written in his old age. How is life different for him on the new reservation? What are his thoughts and memories of the old days, his youth? ★

Crossword Puzzle — *Killer of Death*

ACROSS

1. The main character's name.

5. Gian-nah-tah almost killed him with an _____.

6. Gian-nah-tah's father is a _____.

7. The initials of the leader of the biggest village.

9. _____ Sleeves gave Killer-of-Death his name.

10. The United States and _____ are involved in a border dispute.

12. Killer-of-Death fools the _____ with some gourds.

14. One of the Apache chiefs. (initials)

15. Killer-of-Death feels the white men are _____ to gold.

16. Gian-nah-tah and Killer-of-Death tried to _____ each other.

17. _____ Colorado was a great warrior.

18. _____ and the narrator become friends after the Johnson massacre.

DOWN

2. The narrators little brother.

3. The main characters in this story are _____.

4. Killer-of-Death had to participate in three _____ for his appreticeship.

8. Killer-of-Death would like to marry her.

9. He was given the gray mare that he _____ in a raid.

11. Killer-of-Death dropped one on Gian-nah-tah.

13. The Apache god.

17. The boy had to undergo several tests before he was declared a _____.

40

CRIMSON MOCCASINS

Reading Level 3-4

(A Harper Trophy Book for young readers by Wayne Dyre Doughty. Harper & Row Publishers, Inc., 10 East 53rd St., New York, NY 10022, 1972. $1.95. ISBN no. 06-440015-8.)

Quick Eagle is a Miami youth who learns that he is half white. He makes a foolish mistake during his manhood testing and chooses to starve in the Circle of Shame as punishment. When he leaves the tribe after miraculously surviving the ordeal, he leaves the Indian father he loves, Blue Heron.

Quick Eagle then embarks on a journey which leads him to his white father. He eventually becomes a translator for the U.S. Army and has to face Blue Heron at a peace talk. In his struggle to reconcile his differences with two fathers and two cultures, Quick Eagle learns who he is and what life he must lead.

This is an excellent book for young teens. There is much historical background the students will find interesting and Quick Eagle's conflict with his fathers is one every teenager will identify with. Of importance also is the foolish mistake he makes while trying to please his people. It was a mistake made in all innocence, but it almost cost him his life. The teacher can focus also on ethics and idealism of various characters and human relations.

Questions

PART ONE — RED HAWTHORNE BERRIES — 1777

Chapter One — Day of the Warrior

1. Describe the animals, the plants and weather on this day.
2. What is going to happen to Quick Eagle?
3. How old is he?
4. What is his father's name?
5 .What tribe are they?
6. How long does the manhood testing last?
7. Who is Feather Wind?
8. What does the dog do every day?
9. Why didn't Quick Eagle awaken his father?
10. What is Feather Wind's father's name?
11. What is Quick Eagle's best friend's name?
12. Who is in the hut where the white captives are being held prisoner?
13. Who is Red Feather?
14. What does Quick Eagle want to do to impress Feather Wind's father?
15. Why is it important he do this?
16. What does he do at the river?
17. What does he think about at the river?
18. When Blue Heron wakes up, does he show that he knows what day it is?
19. How does Quick Eagle feel?
20. To what does he compare himself?

Chapter Two — The Chieftan

1. How did Quick Eagle's mother treat him like a child?
2. What does Quick Eagle's mother like to do?
3. What does Quick Eagle say to give his father a clue that he has turned 17?
4. What does Blue Heron say to indicate that he does know?
5. What ritual do they observe as they smoke?
6. What is the Miami way of showing love and respect?
7. What does Blue Heron tell his mother about manhood testing?
8. Why does Blue Heron pull Quick Eagle's braid?
9. What advice does he give him?
10. What does Blue Heron do with the colored pigments (paints).
11. What does each color stand for?
12. What more advice does he give him?

Chapter Three — The Three-Day Race

1. What are some of the people doing when Quick Eagle goes outside that morning?
2. Who is Hard Knot?
3. What is Quick Eagle going to speak to Hard Knot about?
4. What is the magic "trick" One Fire has learned?
5. Who are the Lances?
6. What is Red Panther wearing? Why?
7. What does Quick Eagle plan to bring back with him from his manhood testing?
8. Who kicks Quick Eagle?
9. What does he do?
10. What is the strange feeling Quick Eagle has?
11. What are the warrior societies?
12. What are some of the things the manhood test is supposed to prove?
13. Where does he head for? Why?
14. How does he know his plan will work?
15. What did the British traders call him?
16. What are some of his thoughts as he runs?
17. What is the recurring nightmare he has?
18. What does he think about when he stops to rest for the night?
19. What does he do just before he falls asleep?

Chapter Four — The Judgment

1. Why does he get scared at the stream?
2. What did Many Thunders and the others do?
3. Where did they take him?
4. What does Blue Heron lecture him about?
5. Did Quick Eagle know it was wrong to hide the furs ahead of time?
6. What is his punishment?
7. What did it mean that his friends reached out to touch him on the way to the council lodge?
8. Who saw him bury the furs and turned him into the council lodge?
9. What punishment does Quick Eagle prefer to banishment? Why?

Chapter Five — The Circle

1. What is the Circle of Shame?
2. What is supposed to happen in the circle?
3. How long has he been there so far?
4. What are some things he thinks about?
5. What did the snake say to Quick Eagle?
6. What does Red Panther say about Quick Eagle?
7. What did Red Panther confess to Blue Heron?
8. What would happen if Quick Eagle tried to leave his circle?
9. What did the warriors do so he would get no water?
10. According to Many Thunder, how was Quick Eagle found?
11. When does he leave the circle?
12. What is his new knowledge?

Chapter Six — The White

1. Why is Quick Eagle not killed?
2. Why does his mother scold Blue Heron?
3. What new feelings does Quick Eagle have about his parents?
4. What does Red Panther say?
5. What is Quick Eagle's reaction to this?
6. What does Red Panther offer him?
7. Why does Quick Eagle refuse the present?
8. What happens between Quick Eagle and One Fire?
9. Who does Quick Eagle want to see?
10. Has Blue Heron changed his attitude towards Quick Eagle?
11. What news does Blue Heron have for his son?
12. Why did Quick Eagle leave the lodge so quickly?
13. Where does he go?
14. What does Quick Eagle find out about himself from the white prisoner?
15. Who does he meet under the elm tree?
16. What does Feather Wind want?
17. What is Quick Eagle's reaction?

Chapter Seven — The Snake

1. Describe the scene at the long house.
2. Who were the two strangers?
3. Why have they come?
4. Describe Blue Heron's appearance.
5. Describe the ceremony.
6. What unexpected honor was Quick Eagle given?
7. How does he feel?
8. What does he plan to do the next day?
9. What happens between Quick Eagle and Blue Heron that night?
10. Who comes the next morning?
11. Describe their appearance.
12. What is a kukewium?
13. What message does the lieutenant have from the king?

14. What does the king want Blue Heron to do?
15. How does Blue Heron make the lieutenant angry?
16. Why did Blue Heron return the king's gold medal?
17. Why did Eagle throw down the kukewium?
18. What did they eat at the feast?
19. Why did Quick Eagle charge his father?
20. Why did Quick Eagle drink the Englishman's rum?
21. Why does Quick Eagle say he will have the nightmare no more?
22. Why does Blue Heron treat Quick Eagle with kindness?
23. What does Quick Eagle mean when he tells his father "I will never hurt you again"?

Chapter Eight — Jamison Station

1. What does One Fire want to do?
2. What does Quick Eagle want to do?
3. What are his reasons?
4. Who is he going to take with him? Why?
5. How does One Fire help him?
6. What does he plan to do with the white girl?
7. What is the white man's name?
8. What is the little girl's name?
9. What name does Harm give Quick Eagle?
10. What is Quick Eagle worried about?
11. What does Quick Eagle make Harm Briscoe promise?
12. How does Quick Eagle feel when he sees the fort?
13. What happens when they arrive there?

Chapter Nine — The Finger

1. Where did Quick Eagle live?
2. What did he think of Mitchi Malsa?
3. How did the women and children treat him?
4. What did they do that disgusted him? Why did it bother him?
5. What did Hannah do with his clothes? His moccasins?
6. How is God like the Master of Life?
7. How does one pray to the Master of Life? To God?
8. Who is attacking Jamison Station?
9. Describe Blue Heron's appearance.
10. What does Blue Heron want?
11. What does Jamison want to do with Quick Eagle?
12. What does Harm want to do with Quick Eagle?
13. What does Quick Eagle want to do? Why?
14. What happened when Quick Eagle jumped over the wall?
15. Why have they come for him?
16. What was the lie that One Fire told?
17. What does Blue Heron do and say when Quick Eagle tells him it was a lie?
18. What did Many Thunders say to Quick Eagle?

PART TWO — WHITE HAWTHORN ROSES — 1778

Chapter Ten — Matt Sample

1. Who is the man on the horse?
2. How long has he been gone?
3. What name does Quick Eagle go by now?
4. Where does he live now?
5. What is his job?
6. What are his opinions about the white man's way?
7. How does the Indian live differently?
8. What is one thing John/Quick Eagle liked that white men did?
9. Why does it mean so much to him?
10. Why does he feel he is dying inside?
11. What does John feel about heaven and hell?
12. Who is George Clark?
13. What does Harm think John could do for him?
14. What is John's real name?
15. Which name does he like better?
16. Describe Col. George Clark.
17. What will John have to do if he signs the articles of enlistment?
18. Describe Daniel Cutchen.
19. What did Daniel Cutchen do when John told him that he might be his son?
20. What made him come back?

Chapter Eleven — Passage of the Sun

1. Who does John look like?
2. What is it like between father and son at first?
3. Why does John decide not to tell his father about his Indian life?
4. Why did he want Dan Cutchen's pipe and canoe?
5. Who did John pray for?
6. What does Col. Clark hope he and his men can do?
7. What were some of the hardships they endured?
8. What did the eclipse of the sun mean to John?
9. What does Harm tell Daniel Cutchen?

Chapter Twelve — Kaskaskia

1. Where is Kaskaskia?
2. How does John suggest getting across the river?
3. What kind of Indians are in this area?
4. Why did the men blacken their faces?
5. What does John tell his father about suffering?
6. What does John do to show his father love and respect?
7. How did the men get control of the fort?
8. What did the priest want?
9. What does Col. Clark order John to do?
10. What does John think will happen to him?

Chapter Thirteen — Crimson Moccasins

1. Why was it "insolent" of Col. Clark to stay in the cabin with his men instead of the stockade at Cahokia?
2. What tribes have come for the council meeting?
3. What does John say when Harm asks him what he would do if he had to choose between Blue Heron or the whites?
4. What does John have to do that Clark promised he wouldn't have to do?
5. Which Miami chiefs were present?
6. What happened when John first spoke as translator?
7. What paper did Daniel Cutchen give John?
8. How did this make him feel?
9. What has happened to One Fire?
10. What warning does he bring?
11. What is One Fire's last reminder?
12. What did John dream about?
13. What has John learned from the Master of Life?
14. What choice did Clark give the Indians in his speech?
15. What does the red belt mean?
16. What does the white belt mean?
17. What message of Blue Heron's does Many Thunders tell Clark?
18. Why is Blue Heron going home?
19. What does John/Quick Eagle tell Blue Heron about being white and Indian?
20. What plans does he have for his future?
21. What does "bridge" mean the way he uses it?
22. What do they do together?
23. How does John/Quick Eagle feel about things at the end of the story?

Test

1. What important event is coming up for Quick Eagle?

    a) marriage
    b) manhood testing
    c) adoption

2. The Miami way of showing love and respect is to

    a) touch feet
    b) rub noses
    c) caress the arms

3. Quick Eagle is brought back from his manhood testing in shame because he

    a) hid furs which he was going to trade for a horse
    b) hid food so he would not starve
    c) did not travel far enough away from camp

4. For his punishment Quick Eagle chooses

   a) to be banished from his people forever
   b) to be killed by the Snake Society
   c) to fast in the Circle of Shame until he dies

5. Quick Eagle's feelings about the little white girl are

   a) full of hatred because she is white
   b) disinterested in her except as a hostage
   c) tender and protective

6. Harm Briscoe renames Quick Eagle and treats him like a

   a) son
   b) prisoner
   c) pet

7. Quick Eagle's real name is

   a) John Briscoe
   b) Daniel Cutchen
   c) John Heron

8. Quick Eagle/John's job is as

   a) interpreter
   b) soldier
   c) horse trainer

9. John and Daniel Cutchen

   a) become good friends immediately
   b) never know they are father and son
   c) are like strangers at first

10. Quick Eagle decides to

    a) live the Indian way
    b) be a bridge between white and Indian
    c) live the white way

11. Why did Quick Eagle cheat on his manhood testing?

12. Describe Quick Eagle's feelings for the following people:
    ● Blue Heron
    ● One Fire
    ● Harm Briscoe
    ● Daniel Cutchen
    ● the little white girl

13. What did Quick Eagle have to choose between?
14. Describe Quick Eagle's job with Col. Clark.
15. What does the title of the book refer to?

Activities

1. Draw a picture of Quick Eagle wearing the breechclout described on p. 5. □

2. Draw a picture of Blue Heron as he is described on p. 18. □

3. Find the setting of this story on a map. Draw a map showing where the different events in the story take place. X □

4. Draw the pipe described on p. 19-20 that Blue Heron and Quick Eagle smoke together. □

5. Draw or make a model of Fort Jamison. ★ □

6. Draw or make a model of John's lean-to. ★□

7. Make a character sketch chart or poster depicting the different characters in the book. □✶

8. Design a poster depicting Quick Eagle's two worlds. ✶

9. Was it right to punish Quick Eagle? Was he right in helping the white prisoners escape? Evaluate the justice of the two situations. ○△

10. Write journal entries that one of the following might have written: ★
    - One Fire
    - Blue Heron
    - Harm Briscoe
    - the little white girl
    - Dan Cutchen

11. Write a series of journal entries at different times in the main character's life. Write as Quick Eagle would write, reflecting changes in him over a period of time. ★

12. Write a report on the life of an army scout or interpreter. X

13. Describe Quick Eagle's life as an Indian. Describe his life as a white. Describe his life bridging the two worlds. □○

14. Write an essay in which you explain why Quick Eagle left Blue Heron. ○

15. Write a letter from Quick Eagle to Blue Heron from the white world. ✶

16. Illustrate how different characters dressed. □

17. Describe Quick Eagle's relationship with his mother. X

18. List steps leading to Quick Eagle's banishment. ✓ X

19. Compare your relationship with your parents to Quick Eagle's. ○

Crossword Puzzle — *Crimson Moccasins*

ACROSS

1. The color of Quick Eagle's hair.
5. What One Fire did for him.
7. The main character's Indian name.
8. He did not want to _____ the Articles of War, but he did.
9. _____ Briscoe became like a father to him.
11. Quick Eagle's father was _____ .
12. The little girl was _____ Sample's daughter, Jane.
14. Quick Eagle did _____ want to be banished, he wanted to die.
17. _____ Fire was considered ugly by some, but he was Quick Eagle's dearest friend.
18. The Col. who used Quick Eagle as an interpreter.
20. He fasted in the Circle of _____ .
21. He did not want to _____ white.
22. He was not _____ to be a warrior, he felt.
23. The Station where he lived with Harm Briscoe.
24. Quick Eagle would rather be _____ than disappoint his father, Blue Heron.

DOWN

1. Quick Eagle's Indian father.
2. The Indian name for white men is Mitchi-_____ .
3. He wanted to _____ a bridge between the two cultures.
4. Red _____ was a member of the Lances, a warrior society.
6. Quick Eagle's real father.
10. As part of his manhood testing, he had to particiate in a 3-day _____ .
13. When troubled, he would _____ the Master of Life for help.
14. When told he was to be banished, Quick Eagle cried, "_____! I wish to die!"
15. 14 days alone was part of his _____ .
16. Quick Eagle wanted to be a member of the _____ society of warriors.
19. Another name for weapons and guns.
21. By the end of the story he is no longer a _____ .

WOMAN CHIEF

Reading Level 3-4

(A Laurel-Leaf Book for young adult readers by Rose Sobol. Dell Paperbacks, Dell Publishing Co., Inc., The Dial Press, 1 Dag Hammarskjold Plaza, New York, NY 10017, 1976. $1.50. ISBN no. 0-440-99657-0.)

This novel is a good example of a story based on actual events. *Woman Chief* is based on the diaries of a trader who knew the girl who became chief of the Crow Indians.

Lonesome Star was a young girl who preferred boys' things, especially hunting. Born a Gros Ventre, she was raised lovingly by a Crow warrior after capture during an enemy raid. He encouraged her interests and boyish pursuits.

Lonesome Star eventually earns the right to hunt with the men and later becomes a warrior. Her daring leadership eventually earns her the honor of chief in her village.

It is a lonely life for the woman chief, for most men were in awe of her. She has one friend who eventually becomes her mate, Little Feather.

This novel is an excellent example of a character showing personal courage and goals. There is much violence in the book and it has an unusual ending -- Woman Chief marries Feather Wind, another woman. This and the life Woman Chief has chosen to lead make for some lively discussions on the price one pays if a woman wants to do a man's job. It seems Lonesome Star had to fight for the ERA in her day too.

Questions

Foreword

1. Is the Story based on true events?
2. This is the story of an Indian woman who became _____ .
3. Who wrote the journal that this story was based on?
4. Is the story about the peaceful day-to-day life of the Crows? If not, explain.

Chapter One

1. How old is Lonesome Star at this time?
2. What has she done this day?
3. What did Grandfather give her the night before?
4. What did Lonesome Star expect to happen when she returned with her first kill?
5. What did she feel as she passed the women outside her village?
6. What did she see from the hill overlooking her village?
7. What is her tribe?
8. Who is Chasing Deer?
9. What did he tell her the Crows were going to do?
10. Describe the scene she observes in the village.
11. What happened to Lonesome Star?

Chapter Two

1. How does Lonesome Star feel about crying?
2. What happened to the people in the village?
3. What happened to her grandparents?
4. What was her greatest defense?
5. How did the Crows and the Gros Ventres split up?
6. What was it about the story of the split-up that most interested Lonesome Star?
7. How were the women treated by Crows?
8. Whose family did she go into?
9. How did he treat her?
10. How does Lonesome Star feel about girls' games and duties?
11. What would she prefer to do?
12. What does Sharp Knife tell Lonesome Star to do in order to prove that she can become a hunter?
13. Who is Red Bull?
14. What game are the children playing?
15. How did Lonesome Star capture Red Bull?
16. What do they keep a secret?
17. What did Sharp Knife do that evening?
18. What is the meaning of what he did?

Chapter Three

1. What did Lonesome Star think about?
2. How did Sharp Knife raise her?
3. What did he train her to do?
4. Why was she huddled in the teepee crying?
5. What happens between Lonesome Star and Sharp Knife?
6. What can she do by age 12?
7. What did she accomplish when she was 14?
8. Who were the Hammers?
9. What game did they challenge Lonesome Star to play?
10. What happens during this game?
11. What did Red Bull do that evening?
12. What has Lonesome Star gained by this?
13. What has she lost?

Chapter Four

1. How old is Lonesome Star when she begins hunting buffalo?
2. How is buffalo hunted?
3. For how many years does Lonesome Star hunt buffalo?
4. What did Sharp Knife forbid her to do?
5. Why does she feel unfulfilled?
6. What happened the year Lonesome Star turned 26?
7. Why were the Blackfeet and Cheyenne a menace?
8. How did the Crows act toward the white traders?
9. Why did the Crows need allies?
10. What did the Crows do in the spring and autumn? in the summer? in late autumn? in winter?

11. What happened in 1835?
12. What did Lonesome Star do during the Blackfoot attack?
13. How did she feel afterwards?
14. Why did the Blackfeet signal?
15. Why did Lonesome Star go to speak with the Blackfeet?
16. What did Sharp Knife hand her? What did she use it for?
17. How did she slay the next two warriors?
18. What did the remaining two do?
19. How did the fighting end?
20. What did she tell the sun?
21. What do her last words in this chapter mean?

Chapter Five

1. What action do the Crows want to take against the Blackfeet?
2. How do the Crow people show their grief?
3. What decision did the advisors make in the council meeting?
4. What role will Sharp Knife play in this?
5. What will Lonesome Star do?
6. How did Lonesome Star give thanks?
7. How did the village prepare for the raid during the next three days?
8. What did Sharp Knife give Lonesome Star the night before the raid?
9. What did Little Feather give her?
10. What are Sharp Knife's "misgivings"?
11. What did the scouts find?
12. What did the rest of the war party do?
13. What were some things that went wrong?
14. What is "pemmican"? Why is it bad that it is running low?
15. What news did the scouts bring?
16. Why were the men hopeful again?

Chapter Six

1. How big is the village the Crows decide to attack?
2. Where does Sharp Knife plan to attack from?
3. What do the warriors have to bring them good fortune?
4. What does Lonesome Star have for good luck?
5. Why does Sharp Knife seem sad as he gives attack orders?
6. How many scouts go with him?
7. After hearing gun shots, what do the young braves do?
8. What brave thing did Lonesome Star do?
9. How long did the battle last? What was the outcome?
10. How many horses did they capture from the Blackfeet?
11. Who was killed?
12. What vow had Sharp Knife made before the attack?
13. What happened to save Sharp Knife from disgrace?
14. Describe what happened during the attack.
15. What was Sharp Knife's last act?

16. What was done with his body?
17. What are Lonesome Star's thoughts of her "father"?

Chapter Seven

1. What was Lonesome Star chosen to do?
2. Why did she shoot the gun in the air?
3. What did she do with the blankets? Why did she do this?
4. What did the warriors do while the villagers mourned?
5. What happened on the 11th day?
6. What honor has been bestowed upon Lonesome Star?
7. How did the two warriors fool the Blackfeet?
8. Describe the battle.
9. After they had defeated the Blackfeet, what did Red Bull tell Lonesome Star to do?
10. How did she feel about what she did?
11. How did the village celebrate their victory that night?
12. What was bothering Lonesome Star so that she couldn't sleep? Why did this bother her?

Chapter Eight

1. What did Lonesome Star do within a year?
2. What were the Crow good at?
3. How old is Lonesome Star now?
4. List three types of leaders.
5. What has she accomplished the day before being given her new name?
6. What happened during the ceremony?
7. What name was she given?
8. How does she feel?

Chapter Nine

1. What qualities in a warrior do the Crows admire?
2. What did Woman Chief do with the possessions she acquired in battle?
3. Why was it difficult for Woman Chief to find a husband?
4. What did she do to show that she was available?
5. Who declared her love for Woman Chief?
6. What did Woman Chief kill the next day?
7. What does she plan to do with the hides?
8. How has the white man influenced Woman Chief's thinking?
9. What did Woman Chief give Little Feather?
10. What was done with the white buffalo hide?
11. What happened after the wedding ceremony?

Chapter Ten

1. How do the years affect Woman Chief?
2. How has the white man changed the Crows way of life?
3. How did Rudolph Kurz describe Woman Chief?

4. How do Woman Chief and Little Feather disagree about white men and their new ways?
5. What does Little Feather want Woman Chief to do?
6. What does Woman Chief want to do?
7. What was Little Feather's dream?
8. What was discussed by Woman Chief and the Gros Ventres?
9. When does Woman Chief begin to suspect that she will be trapped?
10. Who killed Woman Chief?
11. How was she killed?

Epilogue

1. What are Little Feather's thoughts of Woman Chief?

Test

1. What happens to Lonesome Star when she is a young girl?
2. What were some of her adventures as a child?
3. What does Sharp Knife encourage her to do?
4. Who is Red Bull?
5. How did Lonesome Star become a hunter?
6. How did she become a warrior?
7. What were some of her accomplishments as a warrior?
8. How did she become a chief?
9. Why was it hard for Woman Chief to find a husband?
10. Who is Little Feather?
11. Describe Woman Chief's last years.
12. How did she die?
13. Did she live a good life? Why or why not?

Activities

1. Write a song or poem about the legend of Woman Chief. ★

2. Do a survey on violence. What do your classmates think? How many acts of violence are in this book? Are they necessary? o∆

3. Make a time line of Lonesome Star's rise to chiefdom. ☐

4. Compare Woman Chief to another woman in politics, such as Golda Meir, Margaret Thatcher, Annie Wauneka, Indira Ghandi or _____. o

5. Find the book mentioned in the introduction and read it. ✔ X

6. Write a report on children's games. X

7. List evidence that Lonesome Star was a compassionate woman. ∆

8. Make something that might have been from the Crow culture. Research their art and culture first. Then make the item and tell about it. □X

9. Analyze Lonesome Star's relationship with her father, Sharp Knife. o

10. Write a report on the American Fur Trading Company, Fort Cass Trading Post or trading posts in general. X

11. Rewrite a scene from Lonesome Star's point of view. What are her thoughts, etc? o

12. Write a different ending for the book. ★

13. Suppose Woman Chief had found the perfect man. What would he be like? ★ o

14. How would Lonesome Star's life have been different if she had not been allowed to play with boys? ★ o

15. Illustrate one of the scenes — playing with Red Bull, fighting the Blackfeet, her wedding, a buffalo hunt, etc. □

16. Research Indian games, then show the class how to play the game. X□

17. Write a journal entry from Edwin Thompson's diary. ★

18. Write an obituary or design a headstone for Woman Chief. ★

19. Write an editorial in which you answer the question — "Should women be leaders?" Δ

20. Was Woman Chief a good leader? Cite evidence from the book. Δ

21. Write a speech that Woman Chief might have made. ★

Crossword Puzzle — *Woman Chief*

ACROSS

4. Main character's name.
8. _____ Bull did not like losing to a girl.
9. Men tried to _____ Woman Chief, but none were successful.
10. This is a _____ story.
11. The American Fur Trading Company built a trading post at Fort _____ .
12. Little Feather had a strange feeling that Woman Chief would _____ if whe went to that strange place.
13. This book was based on E.T. Denig's _____ .
14. Lonesome Star wanted to _____ .
15. Woman Chief's mate. (initials)
18. When whe was little, Lonesome Star lived with her _____ .

DOWN

1. The new name given the main character by War Horse.
2. During the raid by Crows, Lonesome Star was comforted by Chasing _____ .
3. This is the story of a woman who became Chief of the _____ .
5. The warrior who raised her.
6. Lonesome Star's tribe.
11. Lonesome star vowed she would not _____ after her family was killed.
16. The Crows went to _____ with the Blackfeet.

ISLAND OF THE BLUE DOLPHINS

Reading Level 4-5

(A Hans Christian Andersen Medal and Newberry Award-winning classic by Scott O'Dell. Laurel Leaf Library Series for young adult readers, Dell Publishing Co., Inc., 1 Dag Hammarskjold Plaza, New York, NY 10017, 1960. $1.50. ISBN no. 0-440-9400-1)

This novel is a "classic" of its genre. I've had students for whom *Island of the Blue Dolphins* is the only novel they ever read "all the way through".

This is the story of a young Indian girl, Karana, living in the 1800's whose tribe once inhabited an island in the Pacific Ocean. Karana loses her father and many members of her tribe to Aleut hunters. Not long after that, her people decide to leave the island.

Karana's brother, Ramo, is not on board when the ship is set to sail, and while Karana is looking for him, the ship sails without them. Karana's little brother is killed by wild dogs and she is doomed to spend the rest of her life alone on the island. The story is based on a true incident.

This is an excellent story for involvement of the students. Their imaginations are totally captured by Karana's world as year after year she waits for rescue. Meanwhile, Karana becomes immersed in daily activities — her struggle for survival, her search for affection, learning to entertain herself, etc. She learns to hunt, builds a house and makes her own clothes.

Questions

Chapter One

1. What are the girl and her brother doing the day the Aleut ship came to their island?
2. How old is the girl?
3. How old is her brother? What is his name?
4. How does he describe the ocean?
5. Describe the men in the boat.
6. What does the leader say?
7. What is her father's name?
8. What is their tribe?
9. What are the girl's two names?
10. What do the Russian and the Aleut hunters want to do?
11. What bargain does the captain make with the chief?
12. What interrupted the men's discussion?

Chapter Two

1. Describe Karana's island.
2. What warning does Chief Chowig give his people?
3. What news does Ramo bring about Captain Orlov?
4. What does Karana's sister, Ulape, say that she saw?
5. What is the good fortune that came to them?
6. What did the Aleuts want from Karana's father?

Chapter Three

1. How does Karana feel about the seals?
2. What did Karana's father have some men do?
3. What did Captain Orlov's men and women do that showed they were getting ready to leave?
4. What questions did everyone ask themselves?

Chapter Four

1. What are the Aleuts doing?
2. What has Captain Orlov not done?
3. What do Karana and Ulape observe from their hiding place on the ledge?
4. What was in the black chest?
5. What did Chief Chowig want in trade for Otter pelts?
6. What started the fighting?
7. Describe the fighting.
8. What happens to Chief?
9. Why does Karana say he should not have told his name?

Chapter Five

1. How many were killed?
2. What did the survivors do after the storm?
3. Who was chosen as new chief?
4. Summarize what the new chief told the people.
5. What task did he assign to Ulape and Karana? to Ramo?
6. What were some of the tasks assigned to other people?
7. What did Kimki tell the tribe he wanted to do?
8. What is his purpose in doing this?

Chapter Six

1. How long has Kimki been gone?
2. Who has taken his place?
3. What does everyone fear?
4. What message does Nanko have?
5. Why has the ship come?

Chapter Seven

1. Whad did Karana pack in her basket?
2. What did Ulape do?
3. How do Ulape and Nanko tease each other?
4. Why is Nanko in such a hurry to leave?
5. Why is Ramo not on the ship?
6. Why can't the ships wait for Ramo?
7. What did Karana do?
8. Describe how she looked and felt when she reached shore.

Chapter Eight

1. Where did Karana and Ramo spend their first night alone on the island?
2. Where did the sounds of running feet come from?
3. Why is there no food in the village?
4. What do Karana and Ramo gather for food?
5. Why does Ramo hope the ship will never come?
6. What does Karana say she must do before Ramo can be Chief of Ghalas-at?
7. What name does Ramo give himself?
8. Why did Karana stop looking for Ramo the next day?
9. What did she think about instead?
10. What did she hear far off in the distance?
11. What happened to Ramo?
12. What did Karana vow to do?

Chapter Nine

1. What did Karana do the day she decided never to live in the village again?
2. Where did she move to?
3. Why is it a safe place?
4. What does Karana begin collecting?
5. What did she find while digging in the sand?
6. What made it hard to uncover?
7. What was inside?
8. What did Karana do with her treasures?
9. What was a law of her tribe that Karana decided to break?
10. How did she make a spear?
11. How did she make a bow and arrow?
12. What other animals and birds are on the island besides dogs?
13. Describe a typical day in Karana's life now.
14. How long has it been since the ship left?

Chapter Ten

1. Why is Karana unhappy to see winter come?
2. How did she prepare her canoe?
3. How did she keep it on course?
4. What kept her from getting lost?
5. Why is the North star useful to travelers?
6. What happened to the canoe?
7. How did Karana attempt to fix it?
8. Karana cannot decide whether to continue or go back. What does she finally do?
9. What is her first good fortune?
10. What is her second good fortune?
11. How does she feel about the dolphins?
12. What did they do for her?
13. How does she feel when she finally arrives back at her island?

Chapter Eleven

1. What are some things Karana sees that make her happy to be home?
2. How long does she plan to stay on the island?
3. What does she need to do?
4. What kind of place is she looking for?
5. Where does she decide to build her house?
6. What was one thing that made her decide on this place?
7. Why did Karana decide not to build her house on the headland?
8. Why did she decide not to build her house near the old village?
9. What did she do on the third day of rain?

Chapter Twelve

1. How did Karana build a fence for her house?
2. Why did she build the fence first?
3. How did she get in and out of her shelter?
4. What was the legend about trees?
5. Describe Karana's house.
6. What did she eat?
7. How did Karana make a fire last several days?
8. After her house is built what does Karana want to do?
9. What did she use for lamps?
10. Describe the sai-sai and the lamps they became.
11. What kinds of weapons is Karana making?
12. What does she need in order to make a spear?
13. How are bull sea elephants usually killed?
14. Why does this present a problem for Karana?

Chapter Thirteen

1. What is supposed to happen if a woman hunts?
2. Describe the fight of the two bulls.
3. How does Karana hurt her leg?

Chapter Fourteen

1. What happens on the way to the cave?
2. How long does she stay there?
3. How does she fix up her new home?
4. How does she finish her spear?
5. Where does she plan to go?

Chapter Fifteen

1. Describe the leader of the wild dogs.
2. How many dogs does Karana kill?
3. How did she kill the leader?
4. Why couldn't Karana kill the leader?

5. What did she do with the leader?
6. What did she name him? What does the name mean?

Chapter Sixteen

1. What does she begin working on?
2. Describe Karana's relationship with Rontu.
3. What is she going to use the cave for?
4. Describe devilfish.

Chapter Seventeen

1. What does Kanana spend most of her time making?
2. What happens after she hears dogs barking?
3. What happened to Rontu and the other dogs after the fight?

Chapter Eighteen

1. Describe some of the birds.
2. What did Karana do with her birds?
3. What did Karana do so they wouldn't fly away?
4. What did she name them? Why?
5. What did Karana sometimes do?

Chapter Nineteen

1. What does Karana fish for since she hasn't yet captured the giant devilfish?
2. How does Karana finally spear the devilfish?
3. How does she get the fish ashore?
4. How does she keep it from dragging Rontu into the water?
5. How does she finally kill it?
6. Does Karana want to continue hunting devilfish? Why or why not?

Chapter Twenty

1. How does Karana keep seagulls away?
2. What is in Karana's yard?
3. What places does she go?
4. What does Karana plan to do with cormorants?
5. What does she discover at Black Cave?
6. What does she have to do because of the tide?
7. How does she feel about her night in the cave?
8. What does Karana do when she sees the Aleut ships?
9. Where does she spend the night?

Chapter Twenty-One

1. What is a "league"? (use a dictionary)
2. How far (in miles) is the Aleut camp from Karana's cave?
3. Why did Karana think the girl would find her?

4. What did Karana do to occupy her time while she waited for the Aleuts to leave?
5. What did her skirt look like?
6. What happened with the Aleut girl?
7. Why does Karana pack her things?
8. What does she find on her steps?

Chapter Twenty-Two

1. Who is Karana afraid of?
2. Why did Karana decide to stay where she is?
3. What did Karana do for light in her cave?
4. Describe the skirt she made for herself.
5. How did she know the Aleut girl had been near her cave?
6. How did the two girls meet?
7. What is the girl's name?
8. What does "wintscha" mean?
9. Why does Karana prepare to move?
10. What does she find in front of her cave?

Chapter Twenty-Three

1. What is the Aleut girl's name?
2. What words does she teach Karana?
3. What did they do during the meeting?
4. What present did Karana make for her?
5. Why did Tutok stop coming?

Chapter Twenty-Four

1. What did the Aleuts leave behind?
2. How did Karana care for the hurt otter?
3. What did she name the otter? What does this name mean?
4. How did the Aleuts being on the island affect Karana's food and hunting habits?
5. What does she do and think about on sunny days?
6. Describe a typical day in Karana's life at this time.

Test

1. Who came to the island?

    a) Aleuts
    b) Eskimos
    c) Russians

2. Why did Karana's tribe leave the island?

    a) Kimki told them to follow him
    b) Chief Chowig was planning to relocate them
    c) they are afraid the hunters will return and kill more people

3. How did Karana get left on the island?

    a) she didn't hear the signal to board the ship

    b) she was sleeping on the other side of the island

    c) she went to look for Ramo

4. What happened to Ramo?

    a) killed by wild dogs

    b) drowned

    c) sails off to look for his tribe

5. What forbidden thing does Karana learn to do?

    a) pray

    b) hunt

    c) eat meat

6. When she is in trouble at sea, Karana is saved by

    a) a raft

    b) dolphins

    c) a passing ship

7. Karana makes friends with

    a) the leader of the wild dogs

    b) a bull seal

    c) a lost Aleut

8. Karana kills

    a) a dolphin

    b) a wild dog

    c) a giant devilfish

9. Who left her a present?

    a) an Aleut girl

    b) one of her tribesmen

    c) a Russian hunter

10. Her last companion is

    a) a dolphin

    b) a dog

    c) an otter

11. At the end of the story

    a) Karana stays on the island alone

    b) the Aleut girl stays on the island with Karana

    c) Karana leaves with the Aleuts

Activities

1. Draw a picture of a devilfish based on the description in chapter 19. □

2. Draw a picture of Karana's feather skirt. Design some other clothes for her that she could make from available materials. ★□

3. Imagine you were stranded somewhere. Describe the place and your daily life and thoughts. ★

4. Make a schedule for Karana. How should she use her time? Give her some daily things to do that will help her learn the things she is missing from being with her people as well as things that will amuse her or help her survive. ★

5. Write a journal showing entries Karana may have written over the years. ★

6. How could Karana have gotten help or moved to an inhabited island? Did she do all she could to help herself get rescued? o

7. Since this is a true story, find out where the island could have been, which tribe it was, etc. X □

8. Research and report on one of the animals mentioned in the story: X
    - Dolphins
    - Devilfish
    - Wild Dogs
    - Cormorants
    - Seals

9. Write a conversation between Karana and the animals she encounters (supposing they could talk and express their feelings). ★

10. Research and report on the Aleuts. X

11. Rewrite the ending of the story. ★

12. Write a dialogue between Karana and the Aleut girl. ★

13. Draw a picture of Karana's house. □

14. Draw a map/picture of the island. Show where Karana lives, where she did certain things in her book. □ ★

15. Make a model of Karana's house. □ ★

16. Make a small version of Karana's cormorant skirt. □★

17. Design some clothes for Karana to make for herself. ✶

18. Make up a secret name for yourself and explain it. ★

19. Make a shell bracelet similar to the one Karana made for the Aleut girl. ★

20. Compose a song for Karana to sing to amuse herself. ✱

21. Compose a song or write a poem called "The Ballad of Karana." ✱

22. Write some messages Karana could put in bottles to float off. ✱

23. Make a travel book to get visitors interested in the island. Illustrate it, describe the points of interest, activities and accommodations available, etc.   ✱ ☐

24. Draw a series of portraits of Karana to show how she changes over the years. ✱

25. Make a soap carving to represent an ivory carving Karana might have made. ✱

26. Write an essay in which you decide if the ship's leader was wrong to leave without Karana and Ramo. List reasons or justify his actions. Δ

27. Make up some recipes of island food. ★ ☐

28. Make a new invention for Karana to use on the island. ☐ ★

Crossword Puzzle — *Island of the Blue Dolphins*

ACROSS

1. He did not return.

5. Karana made a beautiful _____.

10. The cruel hunters.

11. Captain _____ made a deal for otter pelts.

13. The Aleut girl gave Karana a gift and Karana made her a gift _____.

14. The Aleut word for pretty.

18. It stands for Rest in Peace.

21. Karana's companion.

23. Karana lived in the village of _____-at.

25. Karana and Rontu-Aru often went to _____ Rock in the canoe.

27. Karana's father's secret name.

28. She waited for a _____ to come for her.

30. Most of Karana's food came from the _____.

31. She made a needle out of _____.

DOWN

1. She lived alone for over 18 years.

2. Karana thought, "I know someone will come for _____."

3. It _____ bad luck to tell your secret name.

4. It means son.

6. Ramo thought the island was shaped like a _____.

7. Their home was Coral _____.

8. Karana's secret name.

9. Ramo was killed by wild _____.

12. Karana struggled with a giant devil-_____.

15. Kimki went _____ look for a new home for his people.

16. A cormorant is a kind of _____.

17. Synonym for able or likely.

19. He was not on the ship when it was ready to sail.

20. The Aleut girl.

22. Karana's sister.

24. She decided not to go back into the _____.

26. Karana did not know _____ the strange girl was.

28. Initials of the mission where the Lost Woman is buried.

29. She did not know Ramo was _____ danger.

ZIA

Reading Level 4-5

(A Hans Christian Andersen Award-winning book by Scott O'Dell. Laurel Leaf Library publication for young adult readers, Dell Publishing Co., Inc. 1 Dag Hammarskjold Plaza, New York, NY 10017, 1976. $1.50. ISBN no. 0-440-99904-9.)

In this sequel to *Island of the Blue Dolphins,* Karana's niece and nephew try to find her. Zia and Mando, children of Karana's sister, find a small boat which has washed ashore. They plan to fix it up and search for their long-lost aunt in it. They get advice from Captain Nidever who once made a voyage to the Island of the Blue Dolphins and caught a fleeting glance of Karana.

Zia and Mando, on their voyage out, are taken by whalers who lost the little boat. They finally plan their escape and return to Mission Santa Barbara.

Captain Nidever and Father Vicente set out again , and this time return with Karana. Life is not all that pleasant at the mission for any of them. Several of the children escape and when Karana arrives, she prefers the company of her dog, Rontu-Aru. She too, finally runs away and lives in a cave where she eventually dies, Karana believes, of a broken heart.

Of major interest in this book are the adjustments Karana and Zia must make to mission life. Both miss their homes — Karana's home being her island and Zia and Mando's home in Pala. As a sequel it may not be that satisfying to students who were caught up in Karana's life on the island. Here she is a very shadowy figure whose thoughts we never get to share.

Questions

Chapter One

1. What is the little girl doing with her brother?
2. What is the game they play?
3. What do they find that day?
4. Where do they take it?

Chapter Two

1. What does Father Vicente tell them about the boat?
2. On what page do you find the girl's name first mentioned? What is her name?
3. What do Zia and Mando plan to do with the boat?
4. What is the boat's name?
5. What does Zia make her brother promise?
6. What did Mando make for the boat?
7. What is the new name for the boat?
8. Why did Mando give it this name?

Chapter Three

1. What did Zia and Mando find for their boat while beachcombing?

2. What did they do the following weekend?
3. What was the purpose of this?
4. What did they do the following Sunday?
5. Where does Mando want to go now that the boat is ready to sail?
6. Why do they believe Karana is still alive?
7. Where did Zia live before she came to the mission?
8. Describe Zia's life in Pala.
9. Why did Zia decide to go to the mission Santa Barbara?
10. What has Zia heard about her aunt Karana?
11. Who was the last person to see Karana?

Chapter Four

1. How does Zia get to Captain Nidever's home?
2. What was Captain Nidever doing the morning Zia found him?
3. Why did Zia visit him?
4. How far is it to Dolphin Island?
5. What was the advice Captain Nidever gave to Zia?
6. Why did he give her this advice?
7. What kinds of things will they eat on the voyage?
8. Who are Mukat and Zando?
9. Why did Captain Nidever come the afternoon Zia and Mando were leaving?
10. What did he give them for sailing on rough water?

Chapter Five

1. What island did Zia and Mando come to the day after they left?
2. What did Zia do on the island that she was advised to do?
3. What kind of water animals came to play around the boat while they were sailing?
4. Why weren't the animals afraid?
5. What did Mando think of all during their voyage to the Island of the Blue Dolphins?
6. What do you think pulled the boat? How?
7. What kind of barrel did Mando select for the voyage? Why?
8. What did Zia decide to do after they had been pulled back to Santa Cruz?

Chapter Six

1. Why were Zia's hands numb? What did she do about it?
2. What did Zia warn Mando not to do? Why?
3. What was the size of the big fish that led them around?
4. Describe the marlin.
5. Why do you think the marlin was not afraid of the boat and Zia?
6. Why did Zia cut the line before Mando woke up?
7. What was the first thing Mando notices upon waking?
8. Is he angry? Why or why not?
9. Where are they headed now?

Chapter Seven

1. Where are Mando and Zia now?
2. What does Zia spot while rowing?
3. Describe it.
4. Who is captain now? Why?
5. Why does Mando think that the men will not recognize the boat?
6. What do the men decide to do with them?
7. What is the belief that the men have on the ship?
8. What kinds of jobs are they given?

Chapter Eight

1. Describe the cook.
2. What do the men do on the ship?
3. What is the taboo that the sailors believe in ?
4. Why does the mate believe it is good luck to have women on board?
5. Describe the mate.
6. Where is the crew headed?
7. What made Zia more determined than ever to escape?
8. What do they make from the whales?
9. How did the accident happen?

Chapter Nine

1. What gave Mando and Zia the chance to escape?
2. What kind of job did the captain give Mando after the third day?
3. Explain his new job.
4. What is Zia's plan now?
5. What are Mando's reasons for not wanting to flee from the ship that night?
6. Why is Zia so persistent?
7. What was Zia's reason for leaving her home in the first place?

Chapter Ten

1. Name the items that Zia took with her.
2. Explain how they escape from the ship.
3. How could the watchman have seen them?
4. Why is Mando sad about going back to the mission?
5. What did they discuss while resting on the small boat?
6. How did they get back to Ventura shore?
7. How did the Indians help Zia and Mando?
8. Who came to see them?
9. What did Zia ask Captain Nidever?

Chapter Eleven

1. Where doe Zia see Captain Nidever?
2. Describe the village.
3. When are they planning on leaving?

4. Why is Captain Nidever going?
5. Why is Zia going?
6. What was on Zia's mind for a long time?

Chapter Twelve

1. What does Captain Nidever explain about making a sail?
2. Why did the girls walk along the shore?
3. Why does Zia say she especially loves Father Vicente now?
4. What has Captain Nidever made up his mind about?

Chapter Thirteen

1. What did everyone do to get Father Vicente ready?
2. What did Gito Cruz explain?
3. What did Zia do before nightfall?
4. What kept Zia from going to sleep?

Chapter Fourteen

1. What does the mayordomo "grumble" at?
2. What is Stone Hand's plan?
3. Why does he say they are slaves?
4. What does he give Zia?

Chapter Fifteen

1. Why is Sunday night a good night?
2. What things did Stone Hand do that he was not supposed to do?
3. What does Zia dislike about Stone Hand?
4. What does Zia tell him about her family history?

Chapter Sixteen

1. What happened when the bell in the bit tower struck?
2. What is Father Merced's reaction?
3. What does Captain Cordova say?
4. Who did she pray to? What for?

Chapter Seventeen

1. Why is Zia suspicious of Captain Cordova?
2. Why does Father Merced get upset?
3. Where did the soldiers take Zia?

Chapter Eighteen

1. Describe the room where they put Zia
2. Who is Señora Gomez?

3. What was it like sleeping in a cell?

Chapter Nineteen

1. What does Captain Cordova want?
2. What has he figured out?
3. What is the iron glove?
4. What did Mando do?

Chapter Twenty

1. What is Captain Cordova's "good news"?
2. What is the relationship between Captain Cordova and Father Merced?
3. What does Captain Cordova have?

Chapter Twenty-One

1. What happens the next morning?
2. How does Karana act?
3. Describe the first meeting between Karana and Zia.

Chapter Twenty-Two

1. What bothers Señora Gallegos?
2. What did Karana do when they took Rontu-Aru outside?
3. What did Karana love?
4. What were some things Karana would not do?
5. What did she learn?

Chapter Twenty-Three

1. What things happen while Father Vicente is in charge of the mission?
2. What does Captain Cordova plan to do?
3. Why does Father Vicente go along?

Chapter Twenty-Four

1. Where do Zia and Father Vicente go?
2. Who came with them? Why?
3. What does Stone Hand Say?
4. Why does Rontu-Aru get upset?
5. Why had Stone Hand never sent the message he promised?

Chapter Twenty-Five

1. Why did Father Vicente not mention the group's condition?
2. How did he talk them into coming back?
3. What did Rontu-Aru do?
4. What did Constantino do?
5. What prevented the fire from spreading to the mission and the Corrientes ranch?
6. Why did Mando Head towards the shore?

Chapter Twenty-Six

1. What were the four men arguing about?
2. How is life better with Father Vicente?
3. Discribe the trading ship.
4. Why did everything change suddenly?
5. How did their lives change?
6. What did Karana have to do?

Chapter Twenty-Seven

1. Where did Zia and Mando find Karana?
2. What else is there?
3. Describe the skeleton.
4. Why did Zia bring a medicine man to the cave?
5. What happened to the birds? Why?

Chapter Twenty-Eight

1. What did Stone Head do?
2. What are Mando's plans?
3. How did Zia anger the young priest?
4. What did Karana give Zia?
5. According to Zia, why did Karana die?

Chapter Twenty-Nine

1. Where is Zia going?
2. Why does Father Malatesta think she should stay?
3. Why did Zia never have to put the leash on Rontu-Aru again?
4. How does she feel about going home?

Test

1. This book is a sequel to *Island of the Blue Dolphins*. Sequel means

    a) comes before
    b) comes after
    c) same as

2. Karana is Zia's

    a) sister
    b) mother
    c) aunt

73

3. Zia and Mando build a

    a) boat

    b) hut

    c) gate

4. Captain Nidever saw Karana's

    a) footprints

    b) dog

    c) boat

5. What happened to Mando and Zia on their voyage?

    a) they ran out of food so they turned back

    b) Mando got scared so they turned back

    c) they were pulled back by a large fish

6. They are taken by

    a) a Yankee trading ship

    b) Boston Boy, a whaling ship

    c) a ship of priests on their way to Santa Barbara

7. They finally get back to

    a) Pala

    b) Island of the Blue Dolphins

    c) the mission

8. Who goes with Captain Nidever to Island of the Blue Delphins?

    a) Father Vicente

    b) Father Merced

    c) Zia and Mando

9. Who does not like living at the mission?

    a) Zia

    b) Stone Hands

    c) Mando

10. Stone Hands and several others

    a) refuse to work

    b) make new rules

    c) escape

11. Karana's best friend

    a) becomes Zia

    b) becomes Señora Gallegos

    c) remains Rontu-Aru

12. Father Vicente and Zia

       a) run off to live with Stone Hands
       b) talk Stone Hands and the others into returning
       c) go to Pala

13. Karana moves to

       a) a cave
       b) Pala
       c) back to Island of the Blue Dolphins

14. Karana died of

       a) fever and illness
       b) burns she received in the fire
       c) loneliness and homesickness

15. Describe Zia's life at the mission.
16. Compare and contrast Karana's life on the island with life at the mission.

Activities

1. Research topics: X
   - whales
   - dolphins
   - whaling boats, the whaling industry
   - missions
   - sailboats
   - California Indians   *

2. Write a series of journal entries one of the following people might write: ★ □
   - Karana, on being back "home"
   - Stone Hands, on mission life and injustice
   - Zia, on meeting her aunt
   - Father Vicente, on meeting Karana, running the mission

3. Write an essay in which you tell if you think it was right to bring Karana home. ∆

4. Write an essay in which you tell if you think the children were treated fairly at the mission. ∆

5. Compare and contrast the different Fathers. o

6. Make a sailboat. ✶

7. Write a book report of the novel in which you tell if it was an effective sequel. Why or why not? o

8. Write a different version of Karana's return. ✶

9. Illustrate key scenes from the story such as Karana returning, Karana and Rontu sleeping outside, Zia and Mando making their boat, the fire, etc. ✶ □

10. Write news stories about Karana's return, Stone Hands and the children running away or some other newsworthy events from the book. ★

11. Make a newspaper using the above news stories plus feature stories that might have appeared in a paper at that time. ★

12. Write a conversation Zia might have had with someone about something that happened to her or that she was thinking about. ★

13. How could Karana's life in California have been made better? ∆

SING DOWN THE MOON

Reading Level 5-6

(The Hans Christian Andersen Medal award-winning classic by Scott O'Dell. A Laurel Leaf Library publication for young adults, Dell Publishing Co., Inc., 1 Dag Hammarskjold Plaza, New York, NY 10017, 1970. $1.25. ISBN no. 0-440 -97975-7.)

Sing Down the Moon takes place during the Navajos' Long Walk period. The main character, Bright Morning is a young Navajo girl from Canyon de Chelly. She is kidnapped into slavery by Spaniards. She escapes with the help from her childhood friend, Tall Boy, only to find that soldiers have begun taking the Navajos to Ft. Sumner. Separated from her family, Bright Morning and Tall Boy endure the struggles and hardships of the Long Walk. During this time, she marries Tall Boy, loses her family, raises a baby son and learns what is truly important and valuable in life.

It is suggested that the teacher review with the students the Navajo Long Walk before they begin reading the book. The subject of Navajo slavery may be new to some students and should be discussed also. The settings of the novel and Bright Morning's journey can easily be traced on a map. This book has been immensely popular with students of both sexes and all ages. The teacher might consider recording (or having a student record for an activity) this book on tape as it is an excellent and effective incentive for students slightly below the grade levels mentioned to be able to read along.

Some topics that may or may not be familiar to the students, such as sheep herding, womanhood ceremony, marriage ceremony and healing with herbs, provide excellent opportunities for class discussion and student sharing of personal experience. The locale and the historical background of this book also make it a valuable teaching tool in history and social studies classes.

Questions

Chapter One

1. Why is Bright Morning happy?
2. What happens if you get too happy?
3. What happened to her brother?
4. What did she do a long time ago during a storm?
5. What did her mother do?

Chapter Two

1. Who got to the mesa first?
2. Who else came?
3. What do they joke about?
4. Who is Tall Boy?

Chapter Three

1. What was Tall Boy's first name?

2. When did he change it?
3. Where is he going with the other warriors?
4. What did Running Bird see from the ledge?
5. Where were they from?
6. Who were the Long Knives?
7. What did the soldier tell Old Bear?

Chapter Four

1. Why did Bright Morning put red circles on her sheep?
2. Why is she so excited about the coming spring?
3. Who came to the hogan?
4. What did the girl from Canyon de Chelly know about the men?
5. What happened to the girls?

Chapter Five

1. What did the girls plan to do?
2. What did they refuse to do?
3. What did the girls see the next night?

Chapter Six

1. Which direction are they going?
2. What came to stay with Bright Morning?
3. What did they do with the girls when they got to town?
4. What tribe was the girl?
5. Why was Bright Morning worried about her dog?
6. What was the Nez Perce girl doing?
7. What did she try to say with her eyes?

Chapter Seven

1. Where did the Spaniard take Bright Morning?
2. Who is Rosita?
3. Describe her.
4. Who is the woman?
5. How does Bright Morning act towards them?
6. What happened after the Spaniard left?
7. What does Bright Morning think about?
8. What does the owl mean?

Chapter Eight

1. How did Bright Morning find Running Bird?
2. Who came to the party?
3. How does Rosita like living with the Señora?
4. What does Nehana tell Bright Morning?

Chapter Nine

1. What is a baile?
2. What was supposed to happen 10 days after the baile?
2. What did Rosita tell Bright Morning about Easter?
4. How did Bright Morning get away from the Señora's house?
5. Who was with Nehana?
6. What do they plan to do?
7. Who came to the door of the church?
8. What did they do when darkness came?

Chapter Ten

1. Who did the girls meet on the woodcutter's trail?
2. What did the men say about the horses?
3. When they stopped to eat, Bright Morning saw five figures on the hill. What were they?
4. What did they do so the Spaniards couldn't follow their trail?
5. Did their plan work?

Chapter Eleven

1. When they stop to sleep, who keeps watch?
2. What awoke Bright Morning?
3. Who were the two horsemen?
4. Since they could not outride the Spaniards, what did Tall Boy decide they should do?
5. What happened when the Spaniards caught up with them?
6. What happened to Tall Boy?
7. How many more days was it until they saw their canyon?
8. Why did Bright Morning ride ahead?

Chapter Twelve

1. How did her parents and white Deer react to seeing Bright Morning again?
2. Who went to get Tall Boy?
3. Who was the Medicine Man?
4. What did he have in his bag of curing things?
5. What did he do to Tall Boy?
6. What did it mean when Lapana said Tall Boy would never be able to use his right arm again?
7. What did Bright Morning have to do before shearing her sheep?
8. What kind of ceremony is her mother going to give her?

Chapter Thirteen

1. What is the name of the womanhood ceremony?
2. How did Bright Morning dress?
3. What did she have to do with the corn?
4. What other things did she have to do?
5. What happened on the fifth day?
6. What did Tall Boy say to Bright Morning after the ceremony?

Chapter Fourteen

1. How much time has passed?
2. Who came?
3. What did their paper say?
4. What news did Little Beaver have?
5. Why did Tall Boy want to stay?
6. Where did everyone go?
7. What did Bright Morning see while she was keeping watch?

Chapter Fifteen

1. What did Bright Morning see the next morning?
2. What did the soldiers do on the third day?
3. What did this mean?

Chapter Sixteen

1. How long did their water last?
2. How did they get water the second time?
3. Who died?
4. Where did the father take them?
5. What have the soldiers done to their homes?
6. What happened with the Long Knives?
7. What did they learn about the other Navajos?

Chapter Seventeen

1. Where are the Long Knives taking them?
2. Who did Bright Morning meet from Blue Water?
3. Who did Little Rainbow leave behind?
4. What name was she given?

Chapter Eighteen

1. How many Navajos were on the Long Walk?
2. Who was the second old woman to die?
3. What was it like for the Navajos during this part of their trip?
4. What happened at Bosque Redondo?

Chapter Nineteen

1. What did they have to eat when the food ran out?
2. What other tribe was there?
3. What did the people do that summer?

Chapter Twenty

1. How was the marriage between Tall Boy and Bright Morning arranged?
2. Describe the wedding.
3. Where does Bright Morning want to have her baby?

Chapter Twenty-One

1. What did Bright Morning trade her bracelet for?
2. What did she do with the blankets?
3. How did she save food?
4. What happened with the Apache?
5. What happened to Tall Boy?

Chapter Twenty-Two

1. What adid Bright Morning find hidden in the grass?
2. How did Tall Boy get away from Long Knives?
3. What did Bright Morning and her mother do when they were angry with Tall Boy?
4. How did they leave?
5. What did they do before leaving?
6. Where does Bright Morning want to go? Where do they go?
7. What do they do to make the new place like home?
8. What does she miss?

Chapter Twenty-Three

1. Why did they leave Elk-Running Valley?
2. Where did they go?
3. What did Tall Boy think of sheep?
4. What did Tall Boy see while he was gone for two days?
5. What did Bright Morning hide before she left?
6. What did they find near the cave?
7. What song did Tall Boy sing to his son?
8. Summarize what you learned about the Long Walk from reading the *Postscript*.

Test

1. Who is the narrator of the story?

    a) Bright Morning
    b) Running Bird
    c) White Deer
    d) Tall Boy

2. Bright Morning's brother was killed

    a) when he was hunting, by another hunter
    b) when he fell off a cliff
    c) by lightning for being too happy about killing a deer

3. When Bright Morning left the sheep during the storm,

    a) they all died
    b) her mother did not speak to her or let her herd sheep anymore
    c) they got lost

4. When did Tall Boy change his name?

    a) after he killed the bear
    b) when he got taller
    c) his father asked him to

5. The soldiers were called Long Knives because

    a) they had guns with knives on the end of them
    b) they were all over 6 ft. tall and carried knives
    c) that was their Indian name

6. The girl from Canyon de Chelly told Bright Morning that the soldiers

    a) were kind to them and would do no harm
    b) used the young Indian girls for slaves
    c) wanted the Indians to stay with their land

7. The Spaniard took Bright Morning

    a) to Ft. Defiance
    b) to a school in a big city
    c) to a house where a lady named Señora Rosita lived

8. More than anything else, Bright Morning loved

    a) her sheep
    b) her mother
    c) her dog

9. A *baile* is

    a) an Indian pony
    b) a fiesta
    c) an old woman

10. Who helps Bright Morning escape?

    a) Rosita
    b) Running Deer
    c) Nehana

11. Who do they meet on the trail?

    a) Tall Boy and another warrior
    b) the Long Knives
    c) Running Bird and White Deer

12. What happened when the Spaniards caught up with them?

    a) they kidnapped Bright Morning again
    b) they killed Tall Boy and his friend
    c) Tall Boy got wounded

13. When they got home

    a) they called in a medicine man for Tall Boy

    b) they called in a medicine man for Bright Morning

    c) Tall Boy and Bright Morning got married immediately

14. Bright Morning's mother gave her

    a) a new lamb

    b) a womanhood ceremony

    c) a new dress

15. What did Little Beaver tell them?

    a) that the soldiers were moving all the Navajos to new land

    b) that the soldiers were killing all Indian women and children

    c) that the soldiers were gone and never coming back

16. Little Rainbow gave Bright Morning her

    a) blankets

    b) food

    c) daughter

17. Ever since Tall Boy's injury, he has been

    a) strong and courageous

    b) weak and shy

    c) unable to walk

18. To get ready for their escape, Bright Morning

    a) hid away little bits of food from each meal

    b) traded her bracelet for blankets

    c) told Tall Boy to go without her

19. Bright Morning wants to go home, but they go to

    a) Bosque Redondo

    b) Elk-Running Valley

    c) Canyon de Chelly

20. When they finally got to their home

    a) there were many sheep left

    b) there was a scraggley sheep with long hair waiting for her

    c) there were no sheep left

21. This book is about

    a) The Long Walk

    b) Battle of Little Bighorn

    c) Battle of the Long Knives

22. What kind of a person is Bright Morning? Tell what she does and what she likes and what happens to her in the story.

23. What kind of a person is Tall Boy? How does his injury change him? How is he different from Bright Morning? Do you think they made a good match?

24. Describe some of the Navajos' experience with the Spaniards, the Long Knives and at Bosque Redondo.

25. How had her home changed when Bright Morning finally returned?

Activities

1. Make a list of all characters in the story and tell a little about each one. Draw a picture of each character or find a magazine picture that "represents" or symbolizes that person. Present your work in chart or poster form. X

2. Research a subject from the book, such as the Long Walk or Navajo slavery. X

3. Write several journal entries that some of the other characters might have written such as Tall Boy, Rosita, the soldiers, etc. Be sure to write from their point of view. ★□

4. Design a book cover for the book. The cover illustration should be something that represents the overall theme of the book or your favorite scene. For example, Bright Morning and Tall Boy going with the others to Bosque Redondo, or Bright Morning in Canyon de Chelly with her sheep. ★

5. Make a scrapbook about the story or make a booklet of the ideas you get from reading and some of the subjects mentioned in the book (such as herding sheep, the Long Knives, the Spaniards taking slaves, the baile, Bright Morning's womanhood ceremony or marriage, etc.). ★□

6. Make a pamphlet with illustrations (or cut out magazine pictures) for each chapter. ★

7. Translate one or more chapters into Navajo (can be done orally). X

8. Write an essay in which you give your opinion about the Long Walk. o ∧

9. Make a map showing where events in the book took place. X□

WALK THE WORLD'S RIM

Reading Level 5-6

(A Harper Trophy Book by Betty Baker. Harper and Row, Publishers, Inc., 10 East 53rd St., New York, NY. 10022, 1965. $1.25. ISBN no. 06-440026-3.)

During the time of the Spanish conquest of Mexico, a young Indian boy from Texas meets the unforgettable Esteban. Esteban and the three Spaniards take Chakoh with them to Mexico, land of many promises for the young boy. Along the way, Esteban and Chakoh share many adventures, meet many different people and become good friends.

Chakoh learns that Esteban is a slave to one of the "men-from-the-sun" and his prejudice against slaves ruins their wonderful friendship. He is unable to see Esteban as he once did; the two grow apart and argue constantly.

As guides on a trip to the legendary Cíbola, City of Gold, Chakoh slowly comes to the realization that he was wrong. Almost at the same time, Esteban meets his tragic death.

With this novel, the teacher can introduce the concept of analogy, helping students to make the transition to literary analysis. During the journey to Mexico and to Cíbola, Chakoh is making a journey into maturity. The journey is fraught with trouble just as Chakoh's journey to maturity is a difficult one. In the beginning he is very idealistic about everything, but his child's point of view soon changes.

Questions

The Years Before

1. How did the soldiers get separated from their ships?
2. Who were the four survivors?
3. How did they manage to survive?
4. What happened to the four men?

One — It Goes Hungry

1. What is the main character's name?
2. What are the four survivors called by Chakoh's people?
3. What tribe is Chakoh?
4. What is his father's name?
5. Describe Esteban.
6. What are some things Esteban told Chakoh about Mexico?
7. What story does Chakoh love to hear over and over?
8. Why can't he concentrate on the story this time?
9. What did his father say about hunting buffalo?
10. Why does his father say there is no food?
11. Why did Chakoh quit speaking to Esteban and the other two señors?

Two — Questions

1. What did Chakoh and Esteban do together?
2. What does Chakoh want to know about Mexico?
3. What are the two Spaniards' names?
4. What does Chakoh learn about the Spaniards' god?
5. What does Chakoh notice about Esteban and Dorantes?
6. What does Chakoh want to do?
7. What did his father decide?
8. What was Chakoh's reason for not telling the men about the cactus fruit?
9. What does Esteban say?
10. What did the father give his son for protection?

Three — Strong Medicine

1. What are the first days of their journey like?
2. What does Chakoh want to know?
3. What does Chakoh say about the slaves?
4. What did he do while the men met with the slaves?
5. What did he need a medicine pouch for?
6. What worries Dorantes about the village of the People who were different?
7. What effect did the tea have on those who drank it?
8. What is Chakoh blamed for?
9. What did Esteban do?
10. What did Chakoh put in his medicine bag?
11. Why are they going north before going south to Mexico?
12. Who are the strangely dressed tribe?

Four — The Buffalo People

1. How are Chakoh and the Men-from-the-Sun treated by the Buffalo People?
2. What will happen if they leave the Buffalo People's village?
3. What might happen if they stay?
4. What happened to Esteban?
5. How has Esteban tricked the Buffalo People? Why?
6. Why is Chakoh afraid of the Buffalo People's medicine man?
7. What does he think he must do?

Five — The Cure

1. Why does Dorantes get angry with Chakoh?
2. How did Chakoh get the medicine man to come?
3. What happened to Esteban that worried Chakoh?
4. What did Chakoh do with the contents of his medicine bag?
5. How did they get the medicine man to leave?
6. What cured Esteban of the Spirit-of-Misfortune?
7. Why does Esteban consider staying with the Buffalo People?
8. What does he have to offer them?
9. How does Esteban entertain the people?

10. How did the medicine man honor Esteban?
11. Where do the gourds come from?
12. Who wants to stay? Why?
13. Who finally goes?
14. What does Esteban tell Chakoh about bullfighting?
15. What are two other names for the River People?
16. What magic thing did they do?

Six — A Profit in Scarecrows

1. Why is the Pima village quiet?
2. What has Chakoh learned to make?
3. What did Esteban make that everyone wanted?
4. What did Esteban give Chakoh to keep until they got to Mexico? Why?
5. What is Cíbola?
6. What does Aunt Maria want?
7. How did the turquoise bring evil to Dorantes and Cabeza and Castillo?
8. What did Esteban and Chakoh do to pass time until the river went down?
9. Who are the "hair faces"?
10. What did the slave raiders do?
11. What does Chakoh see for the first time?
12. Where do the Spanish soldiers take them?

Seven — Mexico

1. Describe some of the things Chakoh saw in Mexico.
2. Why did Esteban have to leave Chakoh for awhile?
3. Who did Chakoh stay with?
4. What did Chakoh eat?
5. What does Chakoh expect to find in Mexico?
6. Who is Marcos de Niza?
7. What did he want Chakoh to do?
8. What does Chakoh think of the Mexicans' god?
9. What prevents the slaves from running away?
10. What new name was Chakoh given?
11. What ceremony changed his whole life?
12. List some ways his life has changed.
13. What are some of the things he is lonely for?
14. How long has Esteban been gone?
15. What is the Viceroy organizing?
16. Who is Cortez?
17. Why is he there?
18. Where does he find Esteban?

Eight — Lord of the Viceroy's Stables

1. Where has Esteban been all the time?
2. Why does Chakoh think he is working there?

3. How have Chakoh's feelings about the Buffalo People changed?
4. What frightens Chakoh about Esteban?
5. What does he do when he leaves the stables?
6. What does he notice for the first time?
7. What does he learn about salt?
8. Why did Brother Solano send him for salt?
9. What did he take to Esteban?
10. What does Esteban say Father Marcos wants to do with Chakoh?
11. How does Chakoh learn that Esteban is a slave?
12. How does he react?
13. What did he say to Esteban?
14. What did Esteban say to Chakoh?
15. How did the argument end?
16. What message does Father Marcos bring to Chakoh?
17. Who is to go with him as the other guide?
18. What confusing thought does Chakoh have?

Nine — Return to the Rim

1. What reasons does Brother Solano give for the Spaniards taking slaves?
2. How did Esteban become a slave?
3. What did Esteban think Dorantes would do for him?
4. What did Chakoh do that night?
5. Who went on the trip to Cíbola with them?
6. How have things changed between Esteban and Chakoh?
7. How do the Pima villages seem different to Chakoh?
8. Have they really changed?
9. What does Chakoh miss?
10. Why does Esteban call Chakoh a fool?
11. What does Esteban do during the night that Chakoh discovers the next morning?

Ten — Quarrels

1. Who are the Gray Robes?
2. Who is The Dark One?
3. Who is sick?
4. Where has Esteban gone?
5. What is their system for messages?
6. Why was Brother Oranato sent back to Culiacán?
7. Why was Chakoh sent ahead alone?
8. Why does Esteban stay ahead of Marcos?
9. What is Esteban carving?
10. What does he plan to do?
11. How does Esteban make Chakoh feel guilty?
12. How does Chakoh change Esteban's mind about going to Cíbola?
13. What unforgivable thing did Chakoh do?
14. Why is Father Marcos in a hurry?

Eleven — The Deserter

1. What news does Aunt Maria have about Esteban?
2. What did Esteban do before leaving the Pima village?
3. What is the reason Chakoh could not admit he was wrong about slaves?
4. What excuse did he find to not admit to himself that he was wrong?
5. Why is Chakoh going to go after Esteban?
6. Who does he go with?
7. When he finally sees Esteban, who is with him?
8. When they meet, what do they talk about?
9. What does Chakoh say that makes them friends again?
10. How has Esteban fooled Chakoh?
11. How does Esteban entertain Chakoh that evening?

Twelve — Cíbola

1. Describe the Cíbolans.
2. What did the Cíbolans do to Esteban?
3. Describe the tragedy that happened the next morning.

Thirteen — "Go With God"

1. What is Chakoh watching from the window?
2. What does he no longer want to do?
3. Why is he sad?
4. What is Coronado going to do?
5. What does Chakoh decide to do?
6. What does he take with him?
7. What "vision" does he see?
8. How does Chakoh honor his dead friend's spirit?

Test

1. Chakoh is from

    a) Texas
    b) Mexico
    c) a Pima village in Arizona

2. Esteban is

    a) Viceroy of Mexico
    b) a Spanish bullfighter exploring the new world
    c) Dorantes' Negro slave

3. Esteban and the three Spaniards are on their way to

    a) California
    b) Mexico
    c) Spain

4. They almost decide to stay with

    a) The Buffalo People
    b) Aunt Maria and the Pimas
    c) The Dark Ones

5. Esteban pretends he has been cured from a mysterious illness by

    a) Chakoh
    b) Dorantes and the Buffalo People's medicine man
    c) the Spirit-of-Misfortune

6. Esteban entertains the village with his impersonation of

    a) a hunter and a buffalo
    b) a bear and elk fighting
    c) a deer and a young warrior

7. What does Esteban leave with Aunt Maria's village?

    a) gold
    b) turquoise
    c) scarecrows

8. In Mexico, Chakoh stays with

    a) some Spanish kings
    b) some soldiers
    c) some priests

9. Chakoh finds out that Esteban is a

    a) slave
    b) Viceroy
    c) priest

10. Esteban and Chakoh are going to guide the Spainards to

    a) a turquoise mine
    b) Cíbola
    c) a Pima fiesta

11. Chakoh and Esteban

    a) become better friends in Mexico
    b) argue and have grown apart
    c) run away

12. The Cíbolans

    a) take Chakoh and the priests prisoner
    b) share their gold and turquoise with the Spanish
    c) Kill Esteban

13. Chakoh

    a) honors Esteban's memory, then goes home
    b) goes to the Buffalo People to bring them Esteban's gift of laughter
    c) goes back to Mexico to be a priest

14. What is Chakoh's feeling about slaves?
15. What changes his attitude?
16. What kind of God does Chakoh believe in?
17. What kind of God does he think the other tribes have?
18. What kind of God does he think Mexico has?
19. What things does Chakoh do in Mexico?
20. What has Chakoh learned from his experience with Esteban? How has he changed?

Activities

1. Research topics: X
    • Spanish influence in Mexico and Arizona/New Mexico
    • Spanish exploration of the Southwest
    • Spanish slavery in the Southwest
    • Cabeza de Vaca
    • Marcos de Niza
    • Coronado
    • Cíbola, the City of Gold

2. Write an essay in which you tell if you think it was right for the Spaniards and Coronado to want to take the City of Gold from the Cíbolans? Explain your opnion. Δ

3. Illustrate your favorite scene; for example, Esteban imitating a buffalo and hunter or Chakoh helping Esteban make scarecrows. ☐ ★

4. Make a scarecrow (a small one for the classroom plants or a large one for a field). ★

5. Make a model of Cíbola, the City of Gold. ★

6. Analyze the friendship between Esteban and Chakoh, its ups and downs, etc. O

7. Compare and contrast their friendship with one of yours. O

8. Write an editorial about slavery. Δ O

9. Write an editorial about prejudice. Δ O

10. Chakoh thought Esteban was weak because he was a slave. List evidence that proves or disproves this. Δ

11. Write a story or play that takes place in the City of Gold. Does Chakoh find the magical wonders there that he expects? ★

12. Describe a day in the life and thoughts of a slave. ★

13. Describe a day in the life and thoughts of a medicine man. ★

14. Write a report about medicine men. **X**

15. Describe the Buffalo People and their culture. **X**

16. Design an advertisement for Esteban's scarecrows. ★

Crossword Puzzle — *Walk the World's Rim*

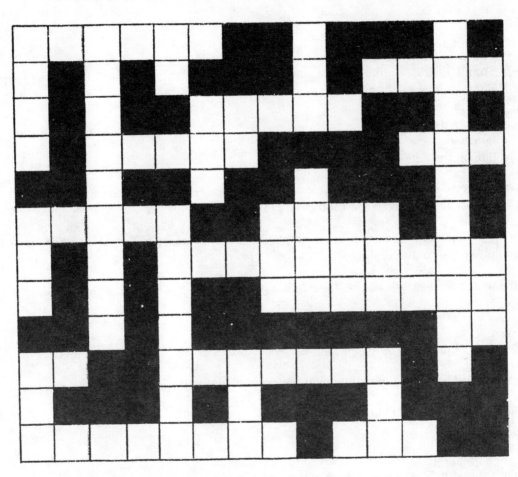

ACROSS

1. Main character's name.

6. Cabeza de _____ was one of the Spaniards with Esbeban.

7. Chakoh and Esteban were asked to guide the Spanish to Cíbola.

9. Where Chakoh was from.

10. "Slaves _____ weak," once thought Chakoh.

11. Chakoh was shocked to learn that Esteban was one.

13. The City of Gold was to make them all _____.

14. Homeland of Dorantes and deVaca.

15. Where the men are headed when Chakoh meets them.

16. "_____ are all that is left of an expedition of 600 men," he said.

17. "___ with God" were Chakoh's last words.

18. Esteban wanted to live with the _____ People.

19. Esteban's "owner."

20. What Esteban drank.

DOWN

1. They wanted the medicine man to think he had performed the _____ .

2. They stayed with her in the Pima village.

3. Esteban was stricken with the Spirit-_____-Misfortune.

4. After Chakoh prayed over Esteban's spirit, he headed for home and he _____ not look back.

5. What Esteban made for the Pimas.

7. Esteban and Chakoh experienced a communications _____ .

8. Brothers Solano and deNiza said, "Stay with _____ ."

11. The four were called Men-from-the- _____ .

12. The Dark One.

13. They went to walk the world's _____ .

17. Chakoh was interested in the Pimas', the Papagos' and the Mexicans' _____ .

19. Another word for enemy.

20. Esteban was called "The Dark _____ ."

FAWN

Reading Level 5-6

(A Laurel Leaf Library publication for young adults by Robert Newton Peck. Dell Publishing Co., Inc., 1 Dag Hammarskjold Plaza, New York, NY 10017, 1975. $1.25. ISBN no. 0-440-92488-X.)

This story takes place in the mid-1700's at Fort Ticonderoga; the British Redcoats and their Mohawk allies fight against the French and their Huron partners. In the middle of this action, Fawn, son of a French priest and grandson of a Mohawk warrior, refuses to take sides.

Because they live in two different worlds, father and son are not aware of the depth of each other's feelings. Fawn deciding how he must live and father and son recognizing their love for each other form the core of this book.

The historical action in this novel is especially lively. One scene involves a daring move on Fawn's part, as he disguises himself and sneaks through the fighting to save his father. He becomes good friends with the young Benedict Arnold, an American soldier. Because Fawn knows people from all four factions — American, British, Mohawk, French — we get a good objective look at the war. For this reason, it is a good book to use in social studies classes.

Aside from the historical background, the teacher can focus on the character and value development of Fawn and his relationships with his father, grandfather and Ben.

Questions

Fort Ticonderoga

1. Describe the history of Fort Ticonderoga.
2. Who are Henri and Old Foot?

Chapter One

1. Why did the boy wait to shoot the deer?
2. What is his name and tribe?
3. Why did Fawn cry?
4. What are some things he did to honor the deer's death?
5. What is the legend Old Foot had told him?

Chapter Two

1. Who is Fawn's father?
2. What did Old Foot call Fawn's father?
3. How did Old Foot and Henri Charbon meet?
4. Why did Fawn's mother and father become man and wife?
5. What does Fawn plan to do with the deer?
6. How was Fawn different from the boys at school?
7. What does Fawn do before going to sleep?

Chapter Three

1. What does Fawn hear?
2. How did Old Foot die?
3. What are some things Old Foot told Fawn about white people?
4. What did Fawn see and hear from the canoe?
5. Why did the last boat drift towards Fawn?
6. What did Fawn think of the young boy rowing?

Chapter Four

1. Which tribe is scouting for the British?
2. What are the three names for the river below the rocks where Fawn is resting?
3. How are the people at Gen. Montcalm's fortress preparing for attack from the British?
4. What does the General teach Fawn?
5. When Fawn returned home, how did he signal his father?
6. What was his reply?

Chapter Five

1. What is Henri Charbon thinking about as he sits on the floor of his bark house?
2. What are his thoughts about his son?
3. What are some of his other thoughts?
4. What has Henri been doing all evening?
5. What does Fawn want Henri to do?
6. What is Henri's reply?
7. What is Fawn going to do?
8. What are Henri's last words to his son?

Chapter Six

1. What did Fawn see as he headed west?
2. What did Fawn do at his father's lodge?
3. What did Old Foot once say about drinking?
4. Who do the three voices belong to?
5. Who have they taken captive?
6. How did two of the Hurons die?
7. What happened to the remaining Huron?

Chapter Seven

1. What is the boy's name?
2. Where is he from?
3. Why did Fawn free Ben?
4. Why does Ben want to be a soldier?
5. How did he get captured?
6. What does Fawn tell Ben about why he saved him?

Chapter Eight

1. What is Ben supposed to do when he has found out something?
2. Why does Fawn climb even higher up the oak tree?
3. Who was Fawn waiting for?
4. Who climbed the tree?

Chapter Nine

1. Why didn't Ben rap on the tree?
2. What has Ben to report?
3. When is the battle to take place?
4. Why does Fawn say "we don't mind death"?
5. What does Fawn want in return for saving Ben's life?
6. What is Ben's whole name?

Chapter Ten

1. How did Fawn get the rabbit?
2. How did Fawn skin the rabbit?
3. What does Henri Charbon dream about?
4. What does Ben dream about?
5. Who is Fawn's only friend?

Chapter Eleven

1. How does Fawn cook his rabbit?
2. What does Fawn say about "land"?
3. What did they drink with "dinner"?
4. What analogy does Fawn use to describe the war?
5. What are Ben's views about "land"?
6. What does Fawn plan to do when his father dies?
7. What is a "flash in the pan"? (give two meanings)
8. What does Ben mean when he says Fawn is *not* a flash in the pan?

Chapter Twelve

1. What are some of Henri's memories from the past?
2. Who is with him?
3. What sound is driving the boy mad?
4. What does the boy want Henri to do?
5. What does Henri do to calm him down?

Chapter Thirteen

1. What are some of the things Fawn sees on the morning of July 8, 1758?
2. What does Fawn remember about his father?
3. How does he plan to get into the fort?

Chapter Fourteen

1. How did Fawn disguise himself as he floated down the river toward the fort?
2. Who is all around him?
3. Where did the ditch lead?
4. Describe the fighting between French and British.
5. Who won the battle?

Chapter Fifteen

1. What feelings about death does Fawn have?
2. Who almost shot Fawn? Why?
3. What happened to the house Henri and Fawn once lived in?
4. What did Fawn dig up?
5. What awakens him?

Chapter Sixteen

1. Who did the footsteps belong to?
2. Why does Henri think Fawn fought with the British against the French?
3. What does Henri feel Fawn has "inherited" from his mother, his grandfather, and father?
4. What has Fawn saved?
5. Why does Fawn refuse to live with the French?

Chapter Seventeen

1. What does Fawn suggest Henri do?
2. What is Fawn going to do?
3. When does Henri finally know that his son loves him?
4. What is the last Henri sees of him?
5. What is a whelp?
6. What does the last sentence mean?

Test

1. Who is the main character? Tell a little about him.

2. What is his father's name? Tell about him.

3. Who is his grandfather? What did he mean to Fawn?

4. How did his grandfather and father meet?

5. Who was his mother?

6. What are some ways that Fawn showed wisdom?

7. Describe Ben and tell a little about their friendship.

8. Who are the British going to attack?

9. Whose side are the Hurons on?

10. How does Fawn get into the fort?

11. Who won the battle?

12. What does Henri want Fawn to do?

13. What is Fawn going to do?

Activities

1. What does the dedication page mean? Read it and write your own interpretation. O

2. Make a model of something described in the book (such as poles on which Fawn carried the dead deer in Chapter Two, a canoe or a fort.) □

3. Research topics: X
   - bagpipes
   - forts
   - the tribes mentioned in the book
   - Benedick Arnold

4. Explain some of Old Foot's words of wisdom. O

5. Interpret some of Fawn's poetic sayings, such as that on p.82. O

6. Look at the map in front of the book. Trace Fawn's entry into the fort. Tell what happened at various spots on the map. X ✓

7. Compare and contrast the different ways of speaking of the following characters — Fawn, Henri, Old Foot, Ben. O

8. Analyze the relationship between Henri and Fawn. O

9. Psychoanalyze Henri Charbon. Why is he unhappily wasting his life? Is going back to France a good solution for him. Why or why not? O

10. Read and interpret the dedication in the front of the book. What does it mean? O

11. Write a report on Fort Ticonderoga/Fort Carillon. X

12. Map out a battle strategy. □ ✶

THE STORY CATCHER

Reading Level — 8 +

(A Spur Award-winning novel by Mari Sandoz. Tempo Books, Grosset & Dunlap, Publishers, New York, 1963. $1.50. ISBN no. 0-448-17054-X.)

This novel has an inconsistent reading level, with passages ranging from 7th to 12th grade levels. The majority however, are on the 7th-8th grade level. A student at those levels will still have occasional trouble because of the inconsistency. The age of the main character and nature of the story make this an appropriate book for younger or below-level readers.

This is the story of a young Sioux who wants to earn respect for his own achievements. Until then he is called Young Lance after his father who won a lance in a show of bravery.

Lance finds a little boy at a battle site whom he takes captive. They become like brothers. Later, when their enemies, the Crows, kidnap the little Ree, Lance risks his life to search for the little boy. He is captured himself and it is during his captivity he finds a special talent for drawing.

Lance escapes with the little boy and the two join his tribe again. Lance loses his mother to smallpox, fights Crows and has to face the possibility of losing the little Ree again, this time to his own people. In the end, Lance keeps his little brother, wins the hand of the girl he loves and is given an appropriate name — Story Catcher. It's good to find a book with a happy ending!

Questions

Chapter One — Little Ree

1. What is the main character's name and tribe?
2. Why has Lance chosen his buckskin horse to ride?
3. What is he looking for?
4. What has happened in this place in the recent past?
5. What does he find there?
6. Who does he encounter at the battle site?
7. What does he do with the little boy?
8. What tribe is the little boy? What does Lance call him?

Chapter Two — The Pit and the Surround

1. What did Lance dream about?
2. What is all the excitement about?
3. Why would it be dangerous if the Rees find out they have the little boy?
4. How does Lance feel about being left behind?
5. What did Lance do while everyone else is off hunting?
6. What do Lance and the little Ree do the next morning?
7. What has Lance been chosen to do?
8. Describe how a buffalo is caught.

9. What happened after they brought the buffalo back?
10. Who was killed?
11. Why did Lance go to the dance?
12. How does he feel about Dawn?
13. What does he do back in his lodge?

Chapter Three — Crow Butte

1. What is everyone busy doing?
2. What do Lance and Deer Foot do?
3. What caused the stampede?
4. What is Lance afraid of?
5. Describe the action with the Crows.
6. Who took the horses?
7. What drawing did the little boy make in the earth?
8. What does it mean?
9. What happened to Lance?
10. Why was he punished?
11. Who is Blue Dawn?
12. Why is he glad she did not see?
13. What happens when they get back to their home?
14. Where does he sleep that night?
15. What does he worry about?

Chapter Four — The Hole

1. How did the boy get to be known as Young Lance?
2. What do his friends want to do?
3. What happens with the Rees?
4. What does he kill for food?
5. Where is his wound?
6. What did he finally do in his hiding place?
7. How does he finally get home?

Chapter Five — In the River Country

1. How has Dawn changed? Why?
2. How does Good Axe feel about Lance returning?
3. Who is shot in the back? Why?
4. What did Lance see in the Loafer village?
5. What happened to the little Ree?
6. How did it happen?

Chapter Six — The Cloudburst

1. How does Lance know the little Ree was probably kidnapped by the Crows?
2. What does he decide to do?
3. What warning did he leave for his people?

4. Who captured Lance? How?
5. Describe his meeting with the little Ree.
6. What does Lance do that interests the Crow women?
7. Why did the Crows dress up and decorate as the camp moved out?
8. How did he escape?
9. How did he find the little Ree?

Chapter Seven — Sun Dance and Bear Butte

1. How has the white man changed things?
2. Why did Sun Shield's village move to the Tongue River?
3. What did Lance do with buckskins?
4. What did he ask of his adviser?
5. What was their decision?
6. Decribe the antelope drive.
7. Where does the village move for the winter?
8. What did Lance do on this trip?
9. What are some of the games the young ones played?
10. How many have come to the annual gathering?
11. What happened with the Old Chief?

Chapter Eight — Hard Winter and the Moose Yard

1. What's wrong with Lance?
2. Who did not survive the illness?
3. What did Cedar give him?
4. Describe Feather Wind's death and funeral.
5. Decribe some of Lance's hardships during the hard winter.
6. Where is he going?
7. What did Lance kill?
8. Who was at the village Lance comes upon?
9. Who is coming for little Ree?
10. Who says Lance is a "man"?
11. Who did Cedar marry?
12. Why does Lance become mournful?

Chapter Nine — A Fight and a Decision

1. What did Pain Maker say about painting?
2. Who are the Sioux going to war with?
3. What makes him want to hurry home to Blue Dawn?
4. Describe the fight with the Pawnees.
5. How was Lance honored by the Brules?
6. What have the Rees come for?
7. What did the chief of the Rees do about the little Ree?
8. What is little Ree's decision?
9. How did Lance know he had been accepted by Blue Dawn's family as her future husband?
10. What new name has Lance been given?
11. Why is this a good name for him?

Test

1. Lance does not have his own
    a) horse
    b) name
    c) bow

2. What does Lance find at the scene of the battle?
    a) a wounded deer
    b) a little boy
    c) a herd of buffalo

3. The village men go off to catch
    a) their enemies
    b) deer
    c) buffalo

4. Lance loves
    a) a little Ree girl
    b) Blue Feather
    c) Blue Dawn

5. The little Ree was kidnapped by
    a) Crows
    b) Sioux
    c) Pawnee

6. Lance has a special talent for
    a) hunting
    b) drawing
    c) fighting

7. Many of Lance's loved ones die because of
    a) illness
    b) attack by Crows
    c) hunger

8. The last battle is with
    a) Apache
    b) Crow
    c) Pawnee

9. The Rees have come for
    a) Lance
    b) the little Ree
    c) horses

102

10. Lance's new name, Story Catcher, was given to him because

    a) he captures a story with his drawings

    b) he was an excellent story teller

    c) he sang of his tribe's battles and adventures

Activities

1. Draw the procession to Bear Butte as described on page 113. □

2. Compare and contrast Lance's friendship with the little Ree to a friendship of yours. o

3. Draw your version of what you think one of Lance's drawings look like. ★□

4. Research the different tribes mentioned in the book. X

5. Report on buckskin art and early American Indian painting. X

6. Get a piece of buckskin leather and paint a picture on it. □✦

7. Write a scene in which you are the little Ree. What are your thoughts as you must decide between the Rees and Lance and his people. ★

8. If you had to earn a name, what would it be? Explain. ★

9. Write a report on one of the following: X
   - smallpox
   - courting rituals of different tribes
   - hunting
   - the Sun Dance

10. What honorable thing did your father do? Compare and contrast him with Good Axe. o

11. Make up some recipes for the foods mentioned on p. 36. □

12. Find out how to make beef jerky. X

13. Make up an ad for the paper for the lost-and-found section for the little Ree. ★

14. Describe and illustrate Lance's wedding. ★□

Crossword Puzzle — *The Story Catcher*

ACROSS

7. He gave Story Catcher his name.
9. Wasna is something hunters _____ .
10. Lance found a little _____ .
12. The two _____ like brothers.
14. Lance is on the _____ of manhood.
15. Lance's friend.
16. Enemy to the Sioux.
17. Feather Woman and many others became _____ .
18. It was feared that _____ would survive
20. Lance's pictures always told a _____ .
21. He took _____ at the buffalo.
22. Lance was invited to _____ .
23. He painted on buck _____ .

DOWN

1. The son of Good Axe.
2. He called him Little Ree, the _____ who is like my brother.
3. Lance wants his own _____ .
4. Lance's tall friend.
5. Sun _____ .
6. Lance's second mother.
11. _____ Axe's other name is Holy Lance.
12. The Sioux hunted a lot of buffalo and _____ .
13. Lance was honored by the _____ village.
14. _____ person gave Dawn words of good wishes at her puberty ceremony
15. Blue _____ rejected Cedar.
17. Many _____ the village got smallpox.
19. Little Ree was about 4 years _____ .
20. Lance was Good Axe's _____ .
21. He wanted _____ Dawn to marry him.

Test and Puzzle Keys

OBJECTIVE TEST ANSWER KEYS

Night At Red Mesa

1 a) 2 c) 3 a) 4 b) 5 a) 6 a) 7 c) 8 b) 9 c)

Killer of Death

1 c) 2 a) 3 c) 4 b) 5 a) 6 c) 7 a) 8 a) 9 c) 10 b)

Crimson Moccasins

1 b) 2 c) 3 a) 4 c) 5 c) 6 a) 7 b) 8 a) 9 c) 10 b)

Island of the Blue Dolphins

1 a) 2 c) 3 c) 4 a) 5 b) 6 b) 7 a) 8 c) 9 a) 10 c) 11 a)

Zia

1 b) 2 c) 3 a) 4 a) 5 c) 6 b) 7 c) 8 a) 9 b) 10 c) 11 c) 12 b) 13 a) 14 c)

Sing Down the Moon

1 a) 2 c) 3 b) 4 a) 5 a) 6 b) 7 c) 8 a) 9 b) 10 c) 11 a) 12 c) 13 a) 14 b) 15 a)
16 c) 17 b) 18 a) 19 b) 20 b) 21 a)

Walk the World's Rim

1 a) 2 c) 3 b) 4 a) 5 b) 6 a) 7 c) 8 c) 9 a) 10 b) 11 b) 12 c) 13 a)

The Story Catcher

1 b) 2 b) 3 c) 4 c) 5 a) 6 b) 7 a) 8 c) 9 b) 10 a)

Arrow to the Sun

```
            J                       B       P O T
      L O R D O F T H E S     U N
            I           A         E           E
S U N       N     A     T     C           B O Y
                  R     H     L           L
M A K E R         R     E     A     C O R N
      I           O     R     Y     R
A     V           W     A Y         O           L I
I     A                             P           I
D     S     S N A K E       W I S E O           O N
N           O           O                       N
            L I G H T N I N G
```

110

Night at Red Mesa

```
D       J     A     D R U M S
I       O     T O O       I
N I G H T               I
E       N         E     K I L L     L
B R O W N         V       N       U
E       Y A Z Z I E     G       J
N     R   B       L             A
A     C O Y O T E       M       N
L     D   X         D E A D
L I K E       T     S     O
Y     O     M O U N T A I N E
      P         O       E
```

Crimson Moccasins

```
B L A C K        M           B
L           P    A      L I E D
Q U I C K E A G L E           A
E           N    S      S I G N     N
H A R M     T    A                  C
E   U   W H I T E                   U
R   N        E           M A T T
N O T   S    R           S         C
O N E   N        C L A R K         H
    S H A M E    R              B E
F I T   K        J A M I S O N
    D E A D      S           Y
```

113

Woman Chief